Secon

Coaching Youth Soccer

A Complete Guide for Coaches, Players, and Parents

Howie Thompson

ISBN: 978-1-60679-010-6
Library of Congress Control Number: 2008934161
Cover design: Studio J Art & Design
Book layout: Studio J Art & Design
Front cover photo: Courtesy of Stephen Dunn/Allsport

Coaches Choice
P.O. Box 1828
Monterey, CA 93942
www.coacheschoice.com

Dedication

In my lifetime, I have coached approximately 2,500 boys and girls. This book is dedicated to each and every player and parent I have had the pleasure of coming in contact with. Without players and parents, the experiences that make up this book would not have been possible. Three of these players, my own children, Jennifer, Chris, and Megan, had probably the toughest road to hoe. Trust me, being the son or daughter of this coach was no walk in the park. They, above all my players, know this.

I have had a modicum of success, which has come my way because I have a wife who keeps me focused and centered on the things that are most important. Jackie has been the one person who keeps me grounded when everyone else around me puts my head in the clouds. It is because of her dedication to me, and to the sport I love, that I was able to dedicate the time and effort that went in to writing this book.

Acknowledgments

The thousands of players with whom I have worked during my three decades of coaching are etched forever in the following pages. But, more than just the players, others helped mold this coach from a young, anxious coach to an older, hopefully wiser, and certainly calmer coach, dedicated to helping young girls and boys love the competition of this game we call soccer. Whitey Budrekas taught me the game that became the way I teach it to younger players. Whitey was Kristine Lilly's high school coach and arguably the best skills tactician in New England. Whitey played for the New York Cosmos in the original men's National Professional Soccer League in America with the great Pelé. It was an honor to learn under his guidance. I am proud to consider Whitey one of my dearest friends.

Foreword

Coaching Youth Soccer is well written, very accurate, and humorous. A fine balancing act is required for the coach of any team between trying to achieve success and pleasing everyone concerned, and there will always be problems, seen and unseen. What is important is how the right balance is gained between doing the best for the children and for the team.

Winning is not everything. How the children progress and learn is the answer. Yet, the coach can only go on the evidence that is presented to him at training and during the games. The other aspect of the players, seen only by their parents, should have no influence on the coach when it comes to making decisions in relation to matches. Parents can be the most helpful people in the world but also the most infuriating. But, the coach can have the children's undivided attention for a certain part of their day, during which the parents are not allowed to enter, and can teach these children a subject of which the parents have no knowledge or experience. These lessons often closely bond the coach and players together so that the relationship becomes special and powerful and trusting. Trust is the reward for a coach and must never be broken.

Well done, Howie. I hope your book is a success. It deserves to be.

Terry Butcher
Assistant Manager
Motherwell FC, Scottish Premier League

Contents

Preface

I hope you will enjoy this book, and I hope that you will gain insight or learn techniques that could help you in the future. If this book helps you develop just one drill, or if you learn one coaching skill you did not already know, I will be happy, and the book will accomplish its task. I had a biology teacher in college, at the University of Tampa, who was a full-blood Cherokee Indian. He always told every class, "If you learn just one thing new every day, you will have learned all you need to know by the time you die." Smart man, and I have tried to live my life by that credo every day.

Have fun, teach the kids as if they were your own, and enjoy every day you have as a coach. It all comes and goes so quickly.

How Soccer Began

God looked around on the seventh day,
And after he rested was heard to say,
"It's a game they need,
One of daring and speed,
A game with a ball
Made for the short and the tall.
One that is fast, where they can throw, kick, and run,
One that can be played in the snow, rain, and sun.
They'll need a field long and wide
And some lines down there to show who's on whose side.
I'll make that ball bouncy, all white and black,
And I'll give them some rules for defense and attack.
There'll be 11 players here and 11 players there,
A goal at each end and some funny uniforms to wear.
I'll keep it quite simple, no hands, just their feet,
And they'll play on a green field where two teams will meet.
They'll learn how to dribble, the ball they will boot,
They'll head, and they'll pass, but most of all shoot.
Now this game I've made, I've created for all,
The young and the old, the short, big, slow, and small.
I think I'll call it SOCCER, just why I haven't a clue,
But I know they will love it, as it's something brand new.
And most of all it's fun as they kick, run, and throw,
And it's something they can keep as they learn and they grow.
So now that I've given a game they can play,
I must go back to resting on this my seventh day.
For the morrow brings a new week and challenges await,
It's Monday morning, and I must turn in the scores before it's too late."

Howie Thompson
Published in CJSA *NewsLine*, 1990
and in the *NSCAA Journal*, 1995

1

Soccer: Roots and Origin

Soccer is the world's most popular sport—whether measured by the number of participants or by the number of spectators. It is played by more than 100 million people in over 150 countries. No one really knows when the game of soccer began. Recorded history traces soccer's origins to ancient Greece, Rome, Egypt, and China. Modern soccer began in England, where the first set of rules was published in 1863 by the London Football Association. Soccer has been played in the United States, in one form or another, for over 100 years, but has only become a major sport since the early 1970s. Depending upon the nation or culture in which the game of futbol (the Spanish spelling) or soccer (as we "Yanks" call it) is played, various styles of play exist: Italian style, Brazilian style, Turkish style, and many more.

The first professional soccer league in the United States was founded in 1967. Through the efforts of world-renowned soccer players, such as Pelé and Kyle Rote, Jr., young boys and girls were introduced to this fast-paced game. Children everywhere began playing with the funny-looking round ball that never bounced the same way twice and was quite difficult to control from one player to the next. Aside from the fact that only approximately 10 percent of the nation knew how to instruct youths in the finer points of the game, kids really enjoyed this new sport.

The lords of our most noble bastions of American sports, such as football, baseball, and basketball, expressed contempt for the "new kid on the block" with negative comments like: "It's just a fad," "It will never catch on," and "It's too difficult." Three decades later, soccer has not only caught on in the United States, but since 1998, the national men's team has been considered one of the top 30 teams in the world, and the women's team was the best team in the world and now ranks as one of the top three. How did this explosion in popularity happen? How did soccer, a team sport that most American men and women knew very little about before 1970, become the sport with the highest percentage of youth participation in America? One, it's a safe sport to play. Few serious injuries occur in soccer, especially in comparison with football. Two, the low cost of fielding a soccer team makes it the logical choice for many youth sports organizations. Shorts, shirts, shoes, and a ball are the only equipment needed. And, three, it's fun!

One of the greatest sports phenomenons of our day is the Americanization of futbol. Soccer is the new frontier of sports. People, from Carlos the skills instructor to Diane the soccer mom, want to be a part of this fast-growing, opportunistic event happening in America. Many men, women, boys, and girls are participating at some level in this sport. Lawyers, doctors, businessmen and women, moms, dads, and even grandparents have caught the wave of this new sports craze.

What does soccer mean? Webster's defines soccer as a form of football played on a field between two teams of 11 players who try to kick a round ball into the opposing team's goal. My definition of soccer is: "A game played on a rectangular field, which is uneven, filled with holes, misaligned, and often located in very remote, hard-to-find places; played by two teams with 11 players each on the field, seven subs who sit on the bench, 30 to 40 screaming adults on the sidelines, two coaches on opposite sides of the field, and three officials, who sometimes actually watch the game; played with a round ball that never bounces the same way twice; and played with the objective to put the ball into the opposing team's goal as many times as possible within the allotted amount of time, or at least until the screaming parents have lost their voices." Anyone who has attended youth soccer games knows this definition very well.

2

Basic Guidelines for Parents and Coaches

During the fall of their children's eighth or ninth year, a group of well-meaning, very enthusiastic parents will approach the local recreation board, or soccer board, and announce, "We have the makings of a great travel soccer team." Notice the word "great." Not good, not even somewhat talented, but "great." This word is an example of problem number one: overexpectations. Even world-famous soccer stars like Kristine Lilly, Tab Ramos, and Pelé were not great at eight years old. Kris was good, not great; she became great because she had outstanding talent and a work ethic second to none.

Why do parents feel the need to pronounce this team of eight-year-olds as "great"? Mainly, because most parents have little or no understanding of what constitutes "good" soccer, let alone "great." They, unfortunately, believe this team will place "small town USA" on the map. That accomplishment can range from being the only team to win a local or regional tournament, to the next state champs, to the next Open Cup champs—perhaps the most coveted title of all youth soccer teams. The Open Cup is a national championship for boys and girls age 14 to 23. But, these parents know that with hard work and good coaching, this eight-year-old travel team, which has yet to have its first practice or play a single game, will be ready to claim their championship title at age 14.

The truth is that this team, composed of approximately 14 eight-year-old players, will have had five skills instructors, four head coaches, and roughly 35 different players by the time the original players are 14 years old. The team will not consist of the same 14 children whose parents are so energetic right now. In fact, only six or seven of the original players will remain together when they start high school at age 14. Why won't these enthusiastic parents stay together and try to keep this group as one? Isn't keeping the team together the goal everyone agreed to when they were eight? Later in the book, you will find out why. For now, the focus is on the coach—the cornerstone to a successful team.

Basic Guidelines for Parents: Choosing a Coach

Parents take an inordinate amount of time choosing the right doctor, dentist, and teacher, but will turn their eight-year-old child over to a man or woman they don't know for an equally important part in a child's development—learning sportsmanship and athletics. Time and time again, parents drop their children off at the first practice without stopping to meet the coach and to learn his level of coaching experience and general philosophy for working with children. A checklist for parents who want to make sure their coach is qualified to instruct their children in soccer, or any other sport, is provided in Table 2-1.

By following this simple checklist, parents will be able to choose a competent, well-rounded coach, one all the parents have met, seen, and agreed upon. After selecting a coach, the next step is to create a parent board for the team. The team parent board will be responsible for providing input regarding tournaments, practice schedules, compensation for the coach, and whether the team needs a skills instructor. The skills instructor can, and should, be the coach, if the coach is talented and not just a parent filling the spot. Typically, the skills instructor is also paid and should meet all of the criteria listed in the coach's checklist (Table 2-1). The age and talent of the team usually determine whether the skills instructor and coach should or should not be the same individual (Table 2-2).

More and more towns and recreation boards are moving to the paid coaches even at the younger ages. Unfortunately, this practice tends not to be beneficial, or necessary, as the younger children need a parental figure on the sidelines and a disciplined figure for teaching aspects. Volunteers should not feel intimidated by the fact that they may not know the sport, since high-quality instructional clinics and licensing courses are available in most communities, and many of them are free or will be paid for by the clubs. Boys and girls alike may not want to see their moms and dads screaming instructions from the sidelines, but they do appreciate it when a parent gets involved in their activities. They may never show it, but most children do love it when their parents help run practice, for example.

- Where has he coached before?
- What level license does the coach hold (D-F for under 12, national or C for over 12)?
- What are the coach's views on playing time?
- Does he have a resume or a coaching biography? Check it out. Make a call to prior teams. Make sure the information is accurate and truthful.
- Has he coached this particular age and gender before, and for how long?
- What does the coach feel are his strengths and weaknesses? Be wary if no perceived weaknesses are cited.
- What is the coach's philosophy on winning and losing?
- What is the coach's three-year goal plan for the team? This question is an important one to ask because some young volunteer coaches may be building a resume. You may want him to coach for one, two, or three years, and you should know his intent.
- What is his greatest soccer achievement? If he won the Amsterdam Cup at the age of 15, his goals for an American team may be a bit lofty at first. If he has never won a championship in his life, he may be the perfect coach to take your child to his maximum potential. (Note: Not every great coach was a good player.)
- Will he explain to the parents how he would run practice? This way, you can get firsthand knowledge of his teaching skills.
- Prior to the initial practice session, have the coach sit down with the players in an informal discussion of team rules, practice, format, and his goals.
- Ask how much he expects, and wants, to be paid. Then tell him how much you are willing to pay. These two figures may or may not be the same.
- Set up a mutually agreed-upon payment system and schedule.

Table 2-1. Coach's checklist

7- to 10-year-olds	Parent coach (volunteer), skills instructor (volunteer/paid)
10- to 12-year-olds Travel	Volunteer coach, paid skills instructor
12- to 14-year-olds Travel	Paid coach/skills instructor
12- to 14-year-olds Premier or Select	Paid coach, paid skills instructors (Note: There should be more than one skills person for specific technique training, such as a keeper coach.)
14- to 18-year-olds Premier or Select	Paid coach, several paid skills instructors

Table 2-2. Guidelines for coach/skills instructor, or coach and skills instructor

Basic Guidelines for Coaches

As the new coach for this group of eight-year-old prodigies, keep your expectations and goals realistic. Remember, they are eight-year-olds; today's speedy wing may well be next year's fullback. The player with the most skill at age eight, or even 10, will often be surpassed by the true athlete in the group by the time they are 12. Success, whether great or small, should never be measured in wins or losses. True success is not the end result but rather the journey traveled along the way. If every day you strive to become better than the day before, the wins and losses will take care of themselves.

When coaching, take baby steps before you run, and enjoy small successes before you win the World Cup. Place your team in situations where they can have the opportunity for success. It is also important that the team learn to fail. For in failure they will learn to appreciate the true rewards of success. No one, in business, sports, or government, has ever been a success without first experiencing failure. Perhaps one of the most glaring examples of this fact is the life of Michael Jordan. Cut from his high school basketball team, he went on to become, arguably, the best basketball player of all time. Dealing with failure is something a coach must learn to handle. Effectively managing your own fears will help teach your players invaluable lessons about handling setbacks.

Fortunately, or many times unfortunately, parents will play an integral part of your soccer coaching experience. Monday mornings will hold a whole new meaning as you go off to your "real" job and face five to six emails from irate parents one week and calls from parents who want to induct you into the Soccer Hall of Fame the next. Billy Martin, ex-coach of the New York Yankees, once said, "Out of every 10 players on this team, I have three who think I walk on water, three who would just as soon spit at me as look at me, and four who just don't give a damn. The secret is to keep the three who hate me away from the four who don't care." That advice is the secret to handling parents.

Every coach discovers that after a season or two, there will be one group of parents who always tell you how well you're doing, a second group who seldom talk to you except to complain, and a third group who never say anything, just show up, cheer, and say "Hi" and "Bye." This last group is the group you want to encourage to mix and mingle with group number one, your supporters. Group three are the swing group. If they commingle with the group that supports you, you're in. If they mix and mingle with the other group, you'll suddenly find yourself in the soccer coaches' unemployment line. You can use the parent board to help mediate situations involving disgruntled parents.

What other pearls of wisdom can help make you the most-liked, most-successful, and most-wanted coach? None. Let nature take its course, and go with the flow. Let

common sense be your guide, and listen to the players, not the parents. You will win, eventually, and you will sometimes lose. But, you must have, and must keep having, fun. Having fun should be the number one goal. If you do not make the soccer experience fun, the players will leave to find something else. Today's children have many more choices than previous generations did, and today's athlete is stronger, faster, and more knowledgeable as well. Overall, they are not as dedicated, but they do want the discipline and the training, and they also want to know "why." You must be prepared to tell them why. Why run laps with a ball and without? Why do push-ups and stretch? Why do cool-downs after a game? Why is a particular drill important? Answer their questions, and they will usually give you maximum effort and their loyalty. Ignore them, and you will be a coach without a team.

3

Guidelines for Coaching and Managing Parents

Not too far into your coaching career (perhaps as early as the second week), you will find that dealing with the kids is fun, teaching them good sportsmanship is fun, and playing the games and going to tournaments is the most fun. But, one element of youth soccer is not fun, no matter where you are or how good or bad your team is—the parents. Three types (or stages) of soccer parents exist, and most, if not all, of the parents go through these stages.

At any given time, you could have one, two, or all three of these types of parents on your team. No sure-fire formula exists for dealing with these "loving, caring, and always-interested-in-fair-play" individuals. However, handling individual parents, and parent groups, in a positive manner is essential to the overall success of the team. The challenge presented by parents is that you're usually not dealing with rational people; you're dealing with individuals who believe that their young sons or daughters are future Olympians or are scholarship-bound for major college programs.

The following true story provides an example. The parents of a nine-year-old girl, Jennifer (not her real name), asked if she should concentrate solely on soccer or diversify her talents and play other sports. Jennifer was a very talented young athlete who had better-than-average vision and speed, as well as size, for her age. She was able to outrun most of the other team members, had the intuition or perception to know what other players would do, and had the ability to change direction "on a dime." She scored goal after goal until about the age of 11, when the other children in the sport began to grow—and Jennifer did not. She only grew a little more until she was 13. Now, her competitors were as fast, if not faster, much bigger, and much more aggressive, as Jennifer was now a bit shy of contact due to her stature. By age 15, Jennifer began to look at other sports like tennis, track, and cross-country, as these were more individual sports, and better suited to her athletic gifts and abilities. Soccer was now her third sport of choice, yet still her love, but she was no longer the "superstar" her parents had once thought she would be. Needless to say, the letters announcing her arrival to the Olympic Training Center and the University of North Carolina were never sent.

Soccer parents can be divided into three different groups: screamers, overachievers, and nonverbal. All three groups come with their own special qualities and characteristics, and each group can both undermine and/or destroy a coach's hard work and efforts if not identified and handled properly.

Screamers

This type of parent can be easily identified, both moms and dads. They will be the ones you can hear from the other side of the field. They begin screaming with the opening kickoff, stop around halftime, begin again with the second-half kickoff, and are out of voice (and breath, thankfully), by the end of the game. "Let's go out there," "Defense," "Kick the ball," "Be aggressive," "Hustle," and "Don't just stand there, do something," are a few of the more tame phrases heard from this motley crew. You also hear: "Hey, ref, are you blind?" "Is your kid on the other team, ref?" "What do they have to do, draw blood?" "You stink!"

When a parent screams and verbally insults the referee, you and the team manager must step in to calm this person down for two reasons: First, and most important, you are teaching sportsmanship to your young, impressionable players, and, second, the referee or official working the game will not tolerate very much of this behavior before removing you as the coach or stopping the game, neither of which is good for the players to experience. What do you do with these types of parents? Review what is acceptable sideline parental behavior, and remind them of the old kindergarten axiom, "If you don't have something nice to say, then don't say anything at all." What works well is to get the team manager to start a system of yellow and red cards (given out by a designated parent at each game). A yellow card is a warning, and a red card is notice to leave the field until composure is regained. This system should be carried out in an attitude of good, clean fun, while sending out the clear message that this type of behavior is completely unacceptable and will not be tolerated. It is amazing how well this system works. It's remarkable how quickly "screamers" can gain control after they've been "carded."

Overachievers

This group of parents is "classic" in youth sports. It's the tennis mom, the baseball dad, and, of course, the soccer mom and dad. These parents all believe they have the next superstar, like the outstanding soccer player from their community who went on to greatness.

Fortunately, in our community we had Kristine Lilly, probably the best defender, now attacker, on the USA Women's National Team, a Gold Medal Olympian, and winner of the first Women's World Cup. Kristine was truly a wonderful athlete from the time she was five years old. On each team, you will always have parents who are absolutely positive they have the next Kristine, but their child either does not live up to the hype or quits the sport due to undue pressure. These parents will do everything and anything they can to help you, which can be perceived as preferential treatment by the other parents. However, because of their enthusiasm to have the "best" for their child, these parents often make a wonderful addition to the parent board. They will find tournaments to play, handle the setup of scrimmages, find the best hotels to stay at while traveling, and will purchase the best uniforms for the kids. But, as the coach, always remember to maintain (and use, if necessary) your veto power so that this group of parents does not begin to "run" the team in your absence. A well-oiled machine runs well because the oil gets to all the parts and not just the main group of pistons.

Nonverbal

The nonverbal parent group is the most dangerous group of parents you will encounter. Unlike the other two types who let you know what they want, this group just quietly watches, takes notes, says very little, and acknowledges even less. They will always be the first ones at the parent meetings and the first ones to leave. Most of the time, they keep to themselves on the sidelines and don't linger to discuss the game with you or other parents. When they do speak, it is usually in time of crisis or tension, and they will be the parents that the rest of the group will listen to. They will either praise you or bury you, and they will be thought of as the parents who are the most knowledgeable. To get this group on your side, you will need to work hard to gain their trust. They should be put in charge of the team budget or given the task of finding the proper skills instructor. They should be on your team parent board so that this board has credibility. This parent group is participating in this particular activity because their child likes it. The minute their child dislikes any part of it, they, and their child, are likely to be gone, usually without notice or fanfare.

Parents are the backbone of youth sports teams and can be a wonderful addition to a successful organization, if you know how to properly handle them. As previously stated, no magic phrases or mystical ways exist for handling a parent group. Rather, plain common sense, logic, and a cool head are the key ingredients for effectively working with your team's parents.

Confrontation is typically not a good alternative for handling problems and should always be used as a last resort. Never get into a heated discussion with a group. One-on-one is a much more advantageous way of handling most parent problems. Always schedule meetings after a practice or on an off day—never before or during practice or before or after a game. Such a meeting will take your attention away from the players, which is not fair to them. If you explain this philosophy up front at your first parents' meeting, you will have very few problems.

The parent meeting is a wonderful opportunity for you and your staff to discuss the workings of the team, the goals of the team, and what you intend to do with this particular group of young athletes. The meeting should last a maximum of one to two hours. Have your manager send the agenda out before the meeting, and stick to the agenda, allowing little or no time for idle chitchat. Following an agenda will move the meeting along, allow enough time to cover what's important, and set the tone for future meetings. Having short, productive meetings will encourage strong parental participation in future meetings. If possible, have someone other than you, such as the team manager, president, treasurer, or a designated parent, run the meeting. Be sure to meet with this person beforehand to help ensure that all goes smoothly.

A typical agenda might look like the following:

- Welcome: Team manager
- Budget or treasurer's report: Team finance person
- Practice times, days, and locations: Team manager
- Team philosophy (expectations, playing time, practice habits, etc.): Coach
- Tournaments: Team manager
- Team structure: Team manager and coach
- Questions
- Wrap-up (coffee and snacks optional)

Having an agenda allows for the business-related items, such as the budget, practices, and team philosophy, to be discussed early, so that other items, like tournaments, team structure, and the ever-popular open-question time, can be held to the end when everyone is eager to leave. Having coffee and snacks at the end will also move the meeting along and give parents a chance to talk among themselves. However, be careful not to let too much mingling occur, because as Billy Martin once said when asked what was so hard about managing the Yankees, "Well, you know, when you have 10 guys sitting on the bench, you're always going to have three guys who hate you, three guys who love you, and four that just don't give a damn. The hardest thing is to keep those three that hate you away from the four that don't give a damn." It would be wise to remember this quote anytime you see three or more parents talking intensely together.

The Parents' Ditty

Parents come in all shapes and sizes.
They scream, they yell, and sometimes they complain.
They bring their kids to games and practices
In the cold, the sun, and even the rain.
Their child is perfect; they never do wrong.
It's always the other parent's child who just doesn't belong.
They want to know why their child isn't playing
As much time as Jimmy or Matt or even Lila and Sue.

It doesn't much matter just how much talent they have,
They want to know right now just what you're gonna do.
They're never quite happy with what you have to say,
And they'll always ask another parent what they think is right.
They'll call the team manager and the league president, too.
And then they'll call you, always very late at night.
A good parent has vision, though sometimes myopic,
And sees only the good things their child has to do.
The rest of the team, well, that's for the coach to handle.
And, you know who the coach is ... that's you.

—Howie Thompson

4

The Organizational Structure of the Team

After tryouts, but before the first practice, you will need to develop the team structure or organization. First and foremost, you must have a team manager, whose job it is to oversee everything. The team manager is responsible for all the administrative duties, so all you have to do is coach. With the team manager's assistance, you will need to identify at least three volunteer parents to make up the parent board. The parent board, the coach, and the team manager should function as an efficiently working board of directors, which can defuse problems, handle policy issues, and determine the philosophy of the team. The board of directors should be created similar to an organization with a president, vice president, and treasurer.

Depending on the team, either Travel or Premier (e.g., Select, ODP, All-Star), the structure will take on slightly different looks. For a Travel team, made up of primarily "in-town" players, your board is easily picked by you and the team manager from those parents who have showed the most interest and involvement. For the Premier group, the board selection now becomes a little more political because you want to have a good mix of people who are interested, people who are knowledgeable, and people who really want to work. You also want to assign jobs and responsibilities so that no one town or region can dominate, making this task even more difficult. Whatever the team, the jobs and their requirements are very similar and look something like the following:

- *President*: The president acts as the spokesperson for the team. He will attend, with the team manager, all town meetings related to the team, and, for the most part, run the parents' meetings. The president is a figurehead in a "Queen of England" sense of the word: his only true power is that he can sign checks if the treasurer is not available.
- *Vice President*: This person handles the parent problems, coaching problems, and field problems, and, in general, must be very knowledgeable about the rules and regulations of soccer. This job would be great for the parent who "knows everything." This person should also be very organized since he coordinates all the details of traveling to tournaments, such as reservations for hotels, restaurants, etc.
- *Treasurer*: Every team has a mom or dad with capabilities or experience in a finance-related field, and ideally, the treasurer position should be held by one of them. The treasurer sets up bank accounts, pays the bills, reconciles the accounts, and gives the budget reports at the parents' meetings. With the coach and the team manager, the treasurer drafts the original budget based on income versus expenses.
- *Team Manager*: This book doesn't have enough space to list everything a good team manager does. He sets up tryouts, distributes roster forms at tryouts, collects forms after tryouts, follows up with parents who don't turn in these forms; types, retypes, and then changes the team roster to be sent to the state, making sure all dates and names are correct; creates and then recreates all passes to be approved by the state association, then picks them up, puts them in alphabetical order on a ring, and holds on to them for safekeeping; has all medical release forms signed, dated, and notarized for tournament play, lines up all the tournaments for approval by the board; sets up all home and away games with other managers; distributes a weekly newsletter that lets the parents and players know everything that was discussed at previous parents' meetings; regularly contacts the coach; makes sure the skills instructors show up on time; and makes sure every player receives a birthday card on their birthday.
- *Coach*: As a board member, it is your job to evaluate talent each season, set up and operate an adequate practice schedule, and coach the team fairly and to the best of your ability. Each season you should hand out a written evaluation of each child's performance noting their strengths and weaknesses. A written evaluation comes in handy at the tryouts each year when you have to "cut" a child and replace him with another. If you cut a child arbitrarily, and with no notice, you are asking for problems. If, however, the parent has seen in writing the child's shortcomings, little or no discussion occurs. Always be honest, and always be fair. Remember that you will often hear things from these children that they would never tell their parents. You will have a unique relationship with them. You can be their friend, but

they have to know where the line is drawn. They—and you—cannot cross it. Coaching can be the most rewarding time of your life, but at times, the most frustrating. Coaching has many ups and downs, but if you love coaching you will find that the good always outweighs the bad.

The most important contributing factor to building a team is to have competent, willing parents to serve as leaders. The most successful teams have 12 to 14 parents of the 18 players involved somehow with the team. And, always follow Billy Martin's advice to keep the three who hate you away from the rest. Put them in charge of securing the nets to the goals. Get them so tired before the games they don't have much to say.

Building a team takes time for players and parents alike. Take your time to organize a group who has now come together for the very first time. You will have parents from different races, religions, and regional backgrounds, parents who have very little knowledge of soccer, and parents who are very knowledgeable about the sport. Stay in control, and make sure that the people you choose for the board are people you can trust to do a good job and to have the best interest of the players at heart. Parent boards will go awry if you don't monitor them and keep in touch with what is happening. It is perfectly acceptable to delegate your authority to a point, but don't delegate your power to veto what you see is going wrong. Remember, you are the only one who is an unbiased adult making decisions. Everyone else has an agenda of some kind.

5

Age-Specific Coaching Guidelines: 7 to 10 Years Old

The 7- to 10-year-olds are, by far, the most fun age group to work with. Why? Because, like an artist, you are working with a clean canvas, and you can create your own masterpiece. Parents' expectations are still within reason, and the officiating is lax enough that the players can still learn without fear of failure. Fun is the key word for this age group. The more fun, the greater the success. If only this statement would still hold true later for these same players.

Between the ages of 7 and 10, boys and girls may play on the same team versus each other, on an all-girls team, or on an all-boys team. (But, by age 9, players are usually divided into single-gender teams.) The key factor for this age group is skill. Skill development and fun should go hand in hand for this age group. It's amazing how much can be learned in a user-friendly atmosphere where the players don't even realize they are learning. Skill development for this age group should consist of the following techniques, which will be discussed later in detail:

- Trapping
- Ball control
- Dribbling with small touches
- Throw-ins

- Controlling a rolling ball
- Playing a dead ball
- Understanding the game

Basic Guidelines for Coaching and Instructing 7- and 8-year-olds

You will notice that "kicking the ball properly" is not on the list of techniques. Many coaches spend hours trying to teach 8-year-olds the proper way to pass, only to have them kick the ball with their toe in a game. You know they will kick the ball with their toe 90 percent of the time, so why bother? Camps, well-intentioned friends, and clinicians will spend days, weeks, and months taking inordinate amounts of the parents' money to teach little Johnny or Sally the proper technique for kicking a soccer ball. If the ball goes where the player wants, it ultimately goes into the net. How it got there does not matter at this age. So, don't waste your time when you can teach these young players so much more.

The first skill on the techniques list is trapping, and rightfully so. If players learn to trap a ball successfully and keep it at their feet, they will be truly successful as they progress to higher levels of play. A successful trap in soccer is one that stays close (less than three yards away) and allows the player to keep control. A good analogy is telling the players to "catch the ball with the feet," thereby creating a helpful image in their minds. Always remind them to trap with whichever foot is coming away from the ball and not toward it so a "soft foot" is created.

Ball control goes hand in hand with trapping, as it's the next step in moving the ball where it should go. Ball control drills are as plentiful as coaches. However, "small touch" drills, which allow players to touch the ball every step while keeping their heads up and not looking at the ball, are preferred. These drills should be approximately 15 to 20 minutes in length and should consist of two to three different drills, moving a group of 20 players through several stations.

Throw-ins can be taught to the youngest players because it is easily taught and learned, and can change the outcome of a youth soccer game. If players are taught the proper way to throw a ball in, they can take control of a dead ball situation and quickly put your team on offense, while the other team just watches. Teaching throw-ins is like teaching a pitcher to throw a baseball or a quarterback to throw a football properly. You start from the ground up and build to a standing throw. Take the time to help each player develop this skill, as it will pay great rewards during game time. This 15-minute drill utilizes all the players and one ball for two players at a time.

Several things can happen when very young players attempt to catch and control a rolling ball, then stop it. They can trip over the ball; they can run right past the ball, never touching it; they can get up to the ball and continue to kick it in the wrong direction; they can run and run and run, never catching the ball, and then fall exhausted to the ground as the ball rolls out of bounds; or they can actually catch and control the ball, at which point, they have to decide what to do with it. The drill to develop this skill is actually quite simple. Break up the group into pairs, have one player roll a ball away from his partner, and have the other one chase it down. Give the instruction to simply catch the ball and stand on it with one foot.

Dead balls are those times in a game when the ball actually stops and is played from a "restart" position. Dead balls occur frequently during the game, and knowing what to do and how to use these "time-outs" to your advantage will make you a wonderful coach. Dead balls occur when the ball rolls out of bounds, a foul occurs, or a goal is made. These dead balls are called one of the following: corner kick, penalty kick, direct kick, indirect kick, goal kick, or kickoff. The word "kick" is used in every instance to indicate that restarting the game must happen with a foot striking the ball. Dead ball drills vary, but repetition is the key, again utilizing all the players, divided into groups of two players as partners with one ball.

You now have 45 minutes to an hour of skill work for your young group to practice each and every session. You are ready to teach them the concepts needed for understanding the game. At ages 7 to 9, the understanding of the game focuses on the most basic of game strategies: we are here, and our goal is there. Tell your players, "We don't want the other team to go here" (showing your net), and "We want our team to go there" (showing the other team's net). It is important to get these young players to understand this most basic part of the game.

Basic Guidelines for Coaching and Instructing 9- and 10-Year-Olds

Now that you have taught your young boys and girls the basics, the next age group is one filled with learning, optimism, and fun. The 9- and 10-year-old athlete can range from one who has great vision, tremendous athletic ability, and a keen sense of the game, to one who can't tie his shoes without pulling a muscle. All of what you have taught your 7- and 8-year-olds must now be retaught to this group and augmented so they don't feel like it has become repetitive and boring. The drills can last longer, and you must keep the entire group involved in what is perceived as a unified skill session, because some of these young players have already been to soccer camps or clinics where they have learned things you have never seen. They have learned the "Maradona," they have been taught how to "mark" as a defender, have picked up buzzwords like "diagonal runs" and "takeovers," and now they know that the center striker is the best position.

What you need to do now is become creative and vary the drills and skills so the group experiences something new every day. Along with the drills mentioned previously, it is now time to introduce some new and exciting skills and drills for the 9- and 10-year-old players.

Trapping is still the primary skill and, believe it or not, will remain so well into players' high school careers. But, now you must encourage the players to "trap and look." Trap and look simply is the same trapping skill described in the previous section, but now players are taught to raise their heads to find an open space, a teammate, or the goal.

Learning to strike a ball properly is a term that most of your players have heard at camp or from some other soccer expert. It is a skill that needs to be worked on at every practice. Couple ball striking with a shooting drill, and you now have incorporated goalkeeper training in your session.

Heading the ball is now introduced as a means of gaining an advantage. Couple heading with throwing and/or long balls/dead balls, or punting practice from the keeper, and you now have a training session to rival the best high school program.

Teaching the tactics of the game now becomes more involved because you want to instruct the players in the "offside" rules, playing with and without the ball, incorporating diagonal runs and takeovers into game play, corner kick drills, goal kick plays, and other dead ball plays. Defense becomes the word of the day, as game scores of 10-7 and 13-12 now become 3-0 or 1-1, and it becomes more important for your players to learn how to play defense. "Goalside, ballside" becomes a phrase you use every day. Teaching technique rather than results begins to become increasingly important.

Certainly, as a first-time experience with this great sport and this age group, the 7- to 10-year-old athletes can be fun, frustrating, and truly the most exciting time of their—and your—life. You might be the very first coach a child has, and he may remember something you say or do forever. Keep in mind that you have the responsibility of teaching these young players sportsmanship, as well as the skills of soccer. They will often mimic your actions, both good and bad, off and on the field. Be a coach and all that goes with that title. Be a friend, a parent, a confidant, and a teacher. Be tough, but be fair, and have rules that everyone must adhere to. Be honest (kids can always spot a phony), and remember to treat every player as if he were your own child. If your son or daughter is on the team, have an assistant coach them and evaluate their talent. Always distribute written player evaluations to the parents at the end of the season. Finally, always remember that soccer is a game. Have fun, have fun, and then when you think the team is ready, have even more fun. Enjoy!

6

Age-Specific Coaching Guidelines: 11 to 14 Years Old

The ages of 11 to 14 can be some of the most exciting times of a young boy's or girl's life as they begin to transition from childhood to young adulthood, move from elementary school to middle school or junior high, and discover that they are now bigger, stronger, faster, and better at most of the things they try—especially athletics. It can, however, also be one of the most challenging times of their lives because they are going through significant physical and emotional changes. Make no mistake, at times you will feel like you're caught in the twilight zone when you try to coach this age group. You'll want to pull your hair out trying to keep this group focused on the tasks ahead. Two totally separate and distinct development levels exist: 11- and 12-year-olds, and 13- and 14-year-olds. Each group presents a unique set of circumstances and challenges.

Basic Guidelines for Coaching and Instructing 11- and 12-Year-Olds

The 11- and 12-year-old soccer players have now grown up, or so they think. Most states now have adopted small-sided play for this age group. In some areas of the country, kids this age play 11-a-side soccer, but for the most part, 8 v 8 is the recommended level of play. In addition, the players (both boys and girls) begin to experience physiological changes that affect athletic performance. For example, boys start to develop greater muscle mass, strength, and power, while girls begin, or soon will begin, menstruation. The male athletes are now able to use their muscles in ways they could not before. They may also have great difficulty controlling their newfound level of strength, oftentimes sending passes way out-of-bounds and shots, which would normally be deftly accurate, into the next zip code. The female athletes may experience significant mood swings that can run the gamut of emotions. Like the males, young women can experience significant improvements in muscle strength and power in response to resistance training.

As stated at the beginning of this chapter, coaching 11- and 12-year-olds can be a most challenging and frustrating time for coaches and players. It can also, however, be among the most rewarding experiences. Coaching this age group allows you to teach more tactics, greater skills and techniques, and actually have a game plan other than kick and run.

For this age group, as with the 7- to 10-year-olds, trapping is at the top of the list of skill development. Ages 11 to 12 are the ideal ages for introducing the "body trap." As with all drills, repetition and repeated practice are critical for ensuring that your players hone this skill. Trapping the ball with the chest and bringing it to the feet is essential for being able to control the mid-level pass or the "50/50 ball."

Tactically, you can now begin to teach your players the importance of a diagonal run and the value of keeping the ball close for control. Teaching the takeover and introducing this age group to corner kick plays and dead ball plays is not only fun, but keeps them advancing on the learning curve.

An arguably more difficult challenge is managing the expectations of your players' parents. Around age 11 or 12, the parents who have had visions of the World Cup for their little Jane or Johnny tend to become more aggressive and demanding. Your only salvation comes when you see your group of talented young soccer players take the ball on their own 18-yard line and make two outstanding touch passes to move the ball out, then your left midfielder makes a diagonal run from the centerline to the opposing 18-yard line, outdistancing three defenders on the way. At the 18-yard line, this wonderful young player now performs a perfect stop dribble, turns the ball back, and crosses it with deft precision to the left wing, who is making a run at precisely the right moment. The left wing traps the ball at his feet, keeping the required three-foot distance away, takes one dribble, then sends what appears to be an accurate shot on goal to the far post. Out of nowhere comes your right wing, who lays out flat in the air and drills the ball into the back of the net like a bullet shot from a gun—*goal*!

This play happened within a two-minute span of time, but it unfolded in front of you as if in slow motion. This kind of play is as good as it gets! After the 1-0 win, your parents and players laud your performance as a coach, and attribute the fine play to your talents and expertise. As you walk off the field, equipment in tow, a small voice behind you calls, "Coach Jones." You turn to see one of your players, the one who is considered #18 out of 18 players, running toward you with a smile, eyes wide with glee, and every muscle in his body announcing joy. "Thanks, Coach. Thanks for putting me in the last 10 minutes to play. I know the parents didn't want me to play. If you didn't have faith in me, I never could have put my head on the ball and scored that goal. I just wanted to let you know how much it meant to me that you had faith in me." As he gives you a high five and turns to walk away, you pick up your bags of balls, throw them over your shoulder, adjust your sunglasses, and wipe a tear off your cheek. Now you know why you coach; now you understand what it's all about. It's not the wins or the losses nor the parents who want to be bosses, it's about the players, it's about loving competition and teaching your players to love it, and it's about how much fun and rewarding coaching can be. At the end of the day, you can hold your head up high as you pack up your things to go home. You know in your heart you coach for the right and most admirable reason—you do it for all the girls and boys.

Tactically and technically, the boys and girls at age 11 and 12 are beginning to realize why they play and why the skills and drills all pay off when they can compete every week. The first touch on the ball is now critical to their success, and progression from "trap and look" becomes "trap and move to space." Small-sided games are the best way to teach about space and touch on the ball. Practice games of 3 v 3 and 5 v 5 with no keepers and small goals become as critical to your teaching methods as do dribbling and shooting.

Practices should be no more than 90 minutes and only 20 minutes should be scrimmage-related. Fitness is essential and most of the players, after a few weeks, will buy into the fitness routine as they will see how easy the last 20 minutes of games become.

Basic Guidelines for Coaching and Instructing 13- and 14-Year-Olds

The difference, the main difference, with both boys and girls aged 13 to 14 is "the opposite sex." At age 12, it was "yucky" to be seen with a member of the other gender. Now, at age 13, and certainly by age 14, in many circles kids may be considered weird if they're not already dating, or at least showing an interest in the opposite sex. This age group can be wonderful, outstanding, and sometimes frustrating to coach. Some coaches even get to the point where they say, "Okay, I'm done. Let's find a 'professional' to handle this group." I find the 13- and 14-year-olds the most enjoyable to coach. Not only do they experience vast and rapid hormonal changes, they also experience rapid improvements in their ability to think, react, and achieve.

Tactical and technical work now becomes very important, whether you are dealing with U-13/14 Premier players or recreational/club players. Your goal as coach is to get these players ready for high school play, if that is where they are headed. By now, most of the players you had when they were 9 or 10 have either gotten more serious about the game or have gone to alternative sports like baseball, football, field hockey, track, swimming, and hockey. Repetition and variation should become part of each training session, with a large amount of time set aside for game play and controlled scrimmage. Controlled scrimmage, as opposed to scrimmage, is where the coach is on the field as a referee/coach. You will stop the game several times throughout each half, noting tactical and technical advantages and disadvantages. Controlled scrimmage is one of the best teaching tools a coach can use—actual game play that can be stopped, positively reinforced, and continued. It's also an excellent way to work on game conditions, corner kicks, dead balls, and penalty kicks. Ideally, controlled scrimmaging should be done every week, sometimes twice a week, depending on whether it's a youth team or a high school team.

By this age, the Premier or Select group in your town will have "stolen" the "best" players from your team, leaving only those interested in playing travel or club soccer. Depending on the area or region, several towns may have to combine teams to keep the less talented players intact together, while the most talented go on to "the next level." Premier, however, often does not mean the best. In most states, the "Premier" concept operates as Select, Level 1, Classic or Tourney Teams. These teams have gotten together for a specific purpose, attracting players with greater talents to a

program that will introduce them to a higher level of play. However, more often than not, it becomes a bidding war (usually somewhere between $1,000 to $2,500) to get players into a program. The contracted commitment for most players is year-round, no participation in other sports or activities is permitted, and the competition for these teams can be fierce. Some coaches and skills instructors are paid $3,000 to $20,000 for a year's work, and budgets that come close to those needed to run small businesses may be used to operate these teams.

At this level, every parent is talking scholarships, and some are being led down a misguided path by less-than-fully-ethical club directors touting the latest and greatest head coach. Some, not all, of these coaches are involved in the big money leagues for two reasons: money and building a resume to get the next bigger and better job. More often than not, these teams are formed for both boys and girls at age 12, and by age 14, the team has changed so much that often the sponsoring town, which had three to four players on the team, is now sponsoring a team with one or no players from that town. Asked why, most parents will tell you that this route is necessary for their son or daughter to gain the exposure needed to be considered for a college scholarship.

The fact is that less than eight percent of all the Premier players countrywide get any kind of financial assistance to play college soccer, leaving over 90 percent playing for the love of the game—the real reason to play. Premier teams advertise that they go to this tourney and that tourney, and that the college coaches will be there watching. The truth is, the college coaches are there mostly to see the U-19 boys and girls. As a

Premier coach, I have never had a call from a college coach regarding a player. However, as a high school coach, who has gotten five players scholarships, I will get calls and letters concerning my high school players every week.

Earlier, it was stated that this age group can be the most enjoyable and rewarding to coach. Why? Why is this group so much fun if you have to deal with all the pressure, competitive situations, and parents? Because of the kids. The 13- to 14-year-old athletes are wonderful to teach. If given a chance, they will perform beyond your wildest expectations. The following story illustrates this point. Late in a game, I subbed in a sometime starter (a sometime sub player who was really coming into her own). I put her in at left wing. With approximately two minutes left, a shot was taken on goal from our right wing. The ball scooted across the goal, and there, all by herself, was our left wing, Debbie, right in the position she should have been, and she touched the ball in for the winning goal. When I attended her Bat Mitzvah, she told me she would always remember that game. I think she will. The fun of this age group can be summed up in one word—the kids. By this age, the kids understand the reason they are playing and really grasp the concept of competing as opposed to winning and losing.

Coaches are teachers who get to wear shorts and T-shirts all the time. You are instructing your class (team) in the finer aspects of sportsmanship, skill, fair play, determination, and competition. You are the link that these players have with the world of sport. You must convey to them every day the love of competition and the meaning of sportsmanship. It is your duty to help these players obtain the skill and know-how they will need to achieve in high school and beyond. You will be remembered more for the things you don't say than the things you do. The things you do out of habit will become the groundwork for your players' work ethics. Your actions will speak volumes over the most verbose dialogue, and your ability to handle defeat with grace and victory with humility will be forever etched in your players' minds and hearts. It is better to be humbled in defeat than remember one moment of your greatest victory.

7

Drills—As Instructional Tools

Soccer drills are like medicine. The proper prescription can help a team in innumerable ways. The soccer coach, however, has the ultimate responsibility to administer the right "medicine" at the right time, in the right amount, and in the right way.

In that regard, all drills should be conducted in a learning atmosphere where every player is given every opportunity to be successful. When athletes do well, they should be praised. When an athlete's performance does not measure up to expectations, that individual should be given constructive feedback that enables that athlete to redirect his efforts in a manner that bring about achieve the desired change.

The technique or skill being stressed in a particular drill should be overemphasized. Coaches should insist and strive for perfection in every drill, by every player, on every repetition.

While many drills can include additional pieces of equipment (e.g., cones), coaches should keep in mind that almost every drill could just as easily be conducted with players used as replacements for any recommended equipment. The one relatively indispensable piece of equipment is a regulation soccer ball. Whenever possible, a soccer ball should be incorporated into the drill, and the pace of actual live action should be simulated.

Finally in my over three decades of coaching, I have come to recognize and appreciate the capability of properly conducted drills to serve as positive coaching tools. In the process, I have attempted to identify what factors seem to have the most meaningful impact on the extent to which a particular drill achieves its intended goals. To the end, I believe that every coach should adhere to the following eight drill axioms:

- *Facilitate success*: When using a drill to teach a specific skill, care and patience must be taken by the coach to insure that the player is successful in the drill. All factors considered, atheletes of all ages learn more quickly when they are successful.
- *Controlled situation*: If it is an offensive drill, the defensive player may defend the action, but should allow the offensive player to be successful. Likewise, if it is a defensive drill, the offensive player may exert counteraction, but should always allow the defensive player to be successful. This factor is very important in creating an environment for success.
- *Pace*: Whatever the general focus of the drill—offensive or defensive—a regulation soccer ball should be used and the pace of actual live action should be simulated.
- *Step-by-step teaching*: The coach must have knowledge of the technique or fundamental that is being taught by the drill. Furthermore, the coach must be able to demonstrate the technique or fundamental being taught. If the coach is unable to perform the required skill, a player who is proficient in the techinique or fundamental should be used to demonstrate the action. The technique or fundamental should be broken down into parts. Such an approach is called step-by-step teaching and can have a very positive impact on the learning process.
- *Be selective*: The coach should pick out a few drills that will teach and simulate the technique or fundamental that is intended to be taught. While variation is needed, the coach should remember that every player must always be made aware of both the purpose of the drill and the technique or fundamental that is being practiced.
- *Emphasize the point*: The technique or fundamental being taught in a drill should always be exaggerated. This step is most easily accomplished in a controlled situation.
- *Teamwork*: An individual drill is where TEAMWORK begins. First, the athletes should be encouraged to listen to the instructions. Second, if a verbal signal is used, they should listen for the command. Third, they should always strive for perfection.
- *Team success*: Individual drills to improve player skills are necessary to TEAM success. Coaches should make sure that every player understands the drill, and why it is necessary, and then create a learning situation for that individual to be successful.

Drills can be exceptional teaching tools. Properly organized and administered, they offer coaches at all competitive levels a constructive resource for bringing out the best in their athletes.

8

50 Nifty Youth Soccer Drills

This chapter includes some basic skills drills that you can use every day and some fun drills that you should try to use every week. Don't try to use all of the drills the first week of practice. You will wear yourself out and confuse the kids. Take your time and slip a new drill in every so often.

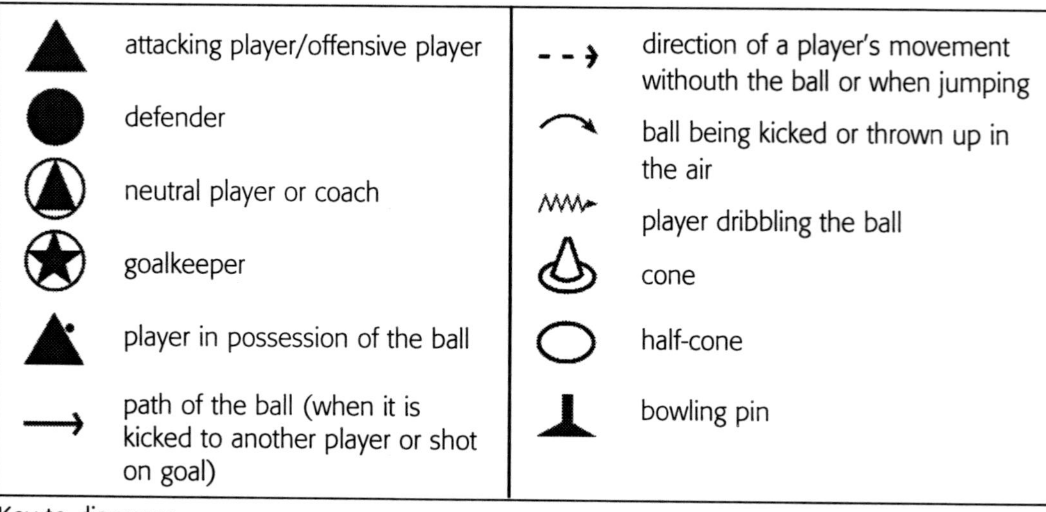

Key to diagrams

Drill #1: Open-Space Demonstration

Objective: To help players recognize how easy it is to move through unoccupied spaces. Use this demonstration to build a base of knowledge about the use of space, and refer to it in later teachings.

Equipment Needed: One ball, two game markers

Description:

Level 1

- Have players huddle in a group.
- Place two markers on a line about 10 yards apart.
- Ask one player to stand by one of the markers.
- Ask that player to walk to the other marker.

Level 2

- Repeat the first two steps from Level 1.
- Ask one player to stand by one of the markers with a ball.
- Ask that player to dribble the ball to the other marker.

Level 3

- Repeat the first two steps from Level 1.
- Ask one player to stand by one of the markers with a ball and another player to stand by the other marker.
- Ask the player with the ball to pass the ball to the teammate who is standing by the other marker.

Coaching Points: You have demonstrated how uncomplicated it is to move, dribble, and pass through open space. Youth players will develop an understanding of space more thoroughly when you give a visual demonstration. Refer to this demonstration often when explaining effecting use of space in training and game situations.

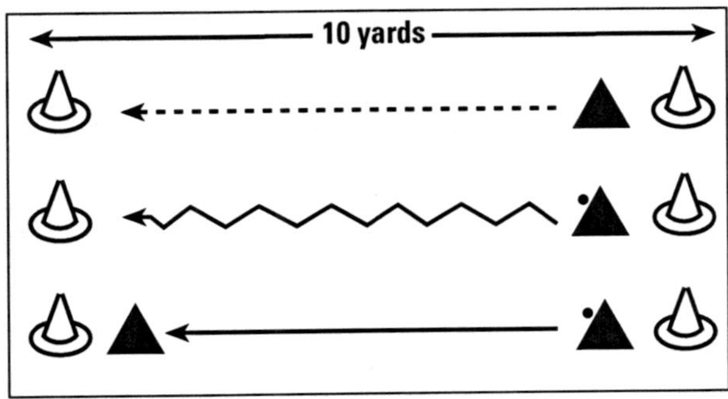

Drill #2: Closed-Space Demonstration

Objective: To demonstrate how impossible it is to move, dribble, and pass through closed spaces.

Equipment Needed: One ball, two game markers

Description:

Level 1

- Have players huddled in a group.
- Place two markers on a line about 10 yards apart.
- Ask player A to stand by one of the markers.
- Ask player B to stand on the line at a point midway between the markers.
- Ask player A to walk on the line to the other marker.

Level 2

- Repeat the first four steps from Level 1, except player A has a ball.
- Ask player A to dribble the ball to the opposite marker without going off the line.

Level 3

- Repeat the first four steps from Level 1, except player A has a ball.
- Ask player C to stand by the unoccupied marker.
- Ask player A to pass to player C.

Coaching Points: At Level 1 player A will find this task impossible because player B, who has closed the space between the two markers, has blocked his pathway. At Level 2 player A will not be able to dribble the ball through the space closed by player B. At Level 3 player A will not be able to pass the ball through the space closed by player B.

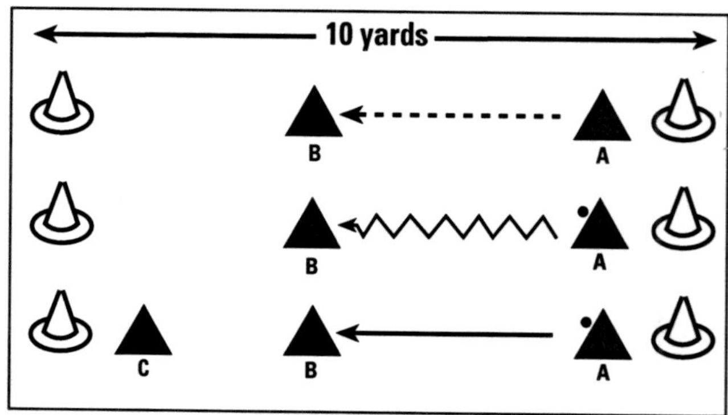

Developing an understanding of open versus closed space (as illustrated in the photos) should be a top priority for youth players. Give players a visual demonstration of how impossible it is to move without the ball, to dribble, or to pass through closed spaces. Refer to this demonstration when players begin clustering, colliding with teammates or opponents, or dribbling and passing into closed spaces. Explain to them the alternative, which is, of course, to use open space.

Open space

Closed space

Drill #3: Personal-Space Demonstration

Objective: To help develop an understanding that personal space is the space that immediately surrounds players and is affected by player movement.

Equipment Needed: Nine game markers

Description:

- Place five players each into four grids, each five yards by five yards. Number the grids 1 through 4.
- Ask the players to move freely through their grids.
- If a player touches another player, he is frozen.
- Ask players from grid number 2 to join the players from grid number 1 and the players from 3 to join the players from grid number 4.
- At this point, all frozen players become unfrozen and rejoin the other players.
- Ask the players to move freely in their grids for about 30 seconds.
- Finally, have all of the players move to grid number 1.
- Ask the players to move freely for about 30 seconds, reminding them not to touch anyone as they move.

Coaching Points: As the players move in a grid with only four other players, maintaining their personal space should not be challenging. As the number of players in a space increases, movement becomes more difficult. When all the players are moving in a small space, it becomes almost impossible to maintain or not invade someone else's personal space. This drill can serve as a visual reminder for players during scrimmages and games of how difficult movement becomes when they cluster. Hopefully, the result will be better spacing and less swarming so that players can maintain personal spaces.

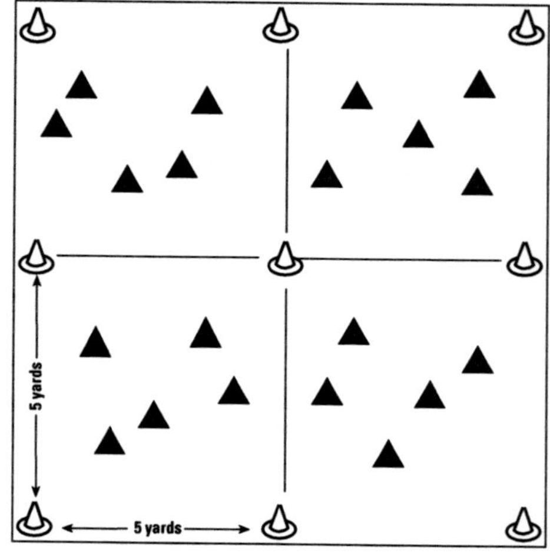

Drill #4: General-Space Demonstration

Objective: To help develop an understanding that general space is the entire area in which a player can function and that within this general space, larger spaces are easier to negotiate than smaller ones.

Equipment Needed: Eight game markers

Description:

- Have all players scattered in a grid identified by four game markers approximately 20 yards apart.
- Ask them to move freely through the entire grid.
- Expand the size of the grid to 50 yards by 50 yards.
- Ask the players to move freely through the larger grid.
- After the players move in both grids, discuss with them in which grid they found it easier to move.

Coaching Points: The personal-space demonstration showed how increasing the number of players in a space affected a player's personal space and movement. This drill demonstrates how increasing the size of the space makes player movement easier because more time is available to make decisions about changing direction, speed, and level. Players should recognize that by using all the spaces within the general space properly, they could maintain field balance and move more freely.

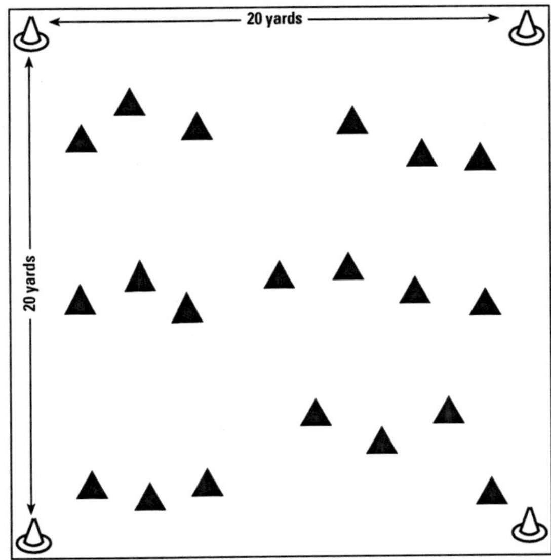

Drill #5: Fancy-Footwork

Objective: To improve the ability to control the ball while in a stationary position with no defensive pressure.

Equipment Needed: One soccer ball for each player, four game markers

Description:

- Scatter players with a ball in a 20-yard-by-20-yard grid.
- While stationary, players practice controlled touches on the ball.
- Players can combine these touches in various ways to change speed, direction, or level. Encourage players to change the position of the ball in relationship to the body with pushaways, pullbacks, rollovers, and so forth.
- Next, have the players change body position in relationship to the ball with stepovers, scissors, walkovers, and so forth.

Coaching Points: There should be time for hundreds of touches on the ball during each practice. Encourage players to explore ways to move the ball using the inside, outside, sole, and heel of each foot. Players may mirror individual moves demonstrated by coaches, but you should encourage them to create new combinations of moves. As players touch the ball, encourage them to maintain good vision constantly. For variety and to reduce fatigue, use partners. Have one partner work on skills for a minute and then give the ball to the partner. Repeat. Change formations using triangles, circles, and so forth to add variety to this drill. It is essential that you give players time to develop these skills from a stationary position, without movement into other spaces, and without defensive pressure. Players should practice these moves at home as part of a daily routine.

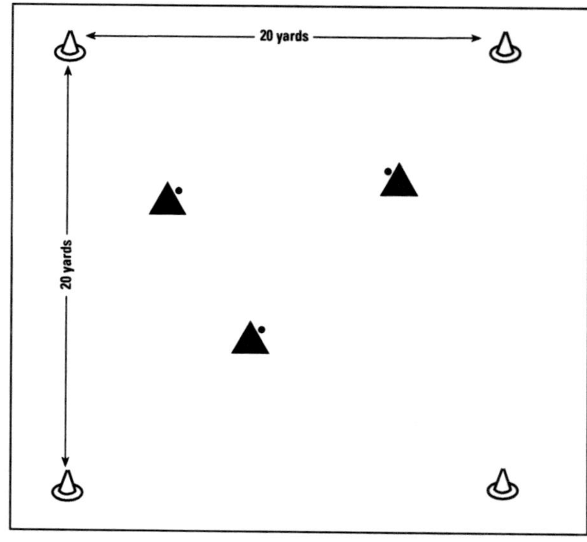

Drill #6: Follow the Leader

Objective: To develop dribbling skills while negotiating space with no defensive pressure.

Equipment Needed: One soccer ball for each player, four game markers

Description:

- Divide group into lines of four or five players in a 20-yard-by-20-yard grid.
- The first player in line is the leader and begins moving through the grid with the rest of the players following while dribbling their balls.
- On the coach's signal, the last person in line will push his ball out approximately five yards in front of the leader, sprint after it, and become the new leader.
- The new last person will repeat this action on the next whistle.

Coaching Points: Coaches should encourage ball control by discussing the relationships of touching the ball with various parts of the foot and proper use of the general space provided so that the lines don't move into the same space. As players become more controlled in their movements, coaches should allow players to do this drill without their signals.

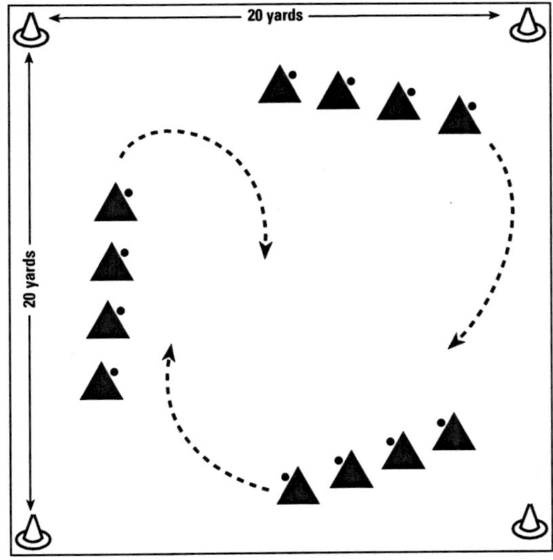

Drill #7: Freedom

Objective: To develop dribbling skills while negotiating space with no defensive pressure.

Equipment Needed: One soccer ball for every two players, five game markers

Description:

- Space partners around a circle approximately 30 yards in diameter.
- On the coach's whistle, the partner with the ball travels into the circle, practicing his individual moves as he encounters other players who are doing likewise.
- After a minute of moving, the player with the ball returns and gives the ball to his partner, who repeats the action.
- Players have complete freedom to use any of their individual moves during this drill.

Coaching Points: Encourage players to use a variety of individual moves to change directions, speeds, and levels as they negotiate space. Refer to the demonstration on space and movement concepts if players are moving into closed spaces. This drill is the next step in the dribbling progression because it requires using individual moves to travel through space. The drill allows players the freedom to develop skills without defensive pressure.

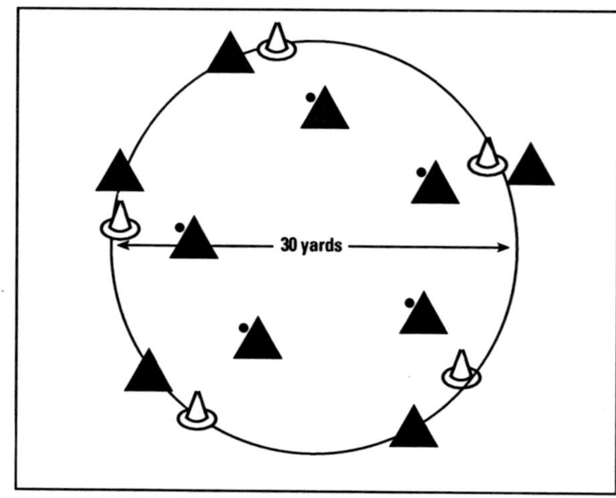

Drill #8: Freeze

Objective: To develop dribbling skills while negotiating space with no defensive pressure.

Equipment Needed: One soccer ball for each player, four game markers

Description:

- Scatter players in a 20-yard-by-20-yard grid.
- All players move freely with a ball through the grid.
- When the coach signals by blowing a whistle, the players must freeze by bringing their balls to a complete stop.
- Variations of this drill might include touching the ball with any body part on one side of the body, freezing on a specific number of body parts, or freezing at various levels.

Coaching Points: This drill allows players to develop individual moves while negotiating space without defensive pressure. Encourage players to use body parts on their nondominant side. Freezing at various levels might include straight leg, crouched, or kneeling positions.

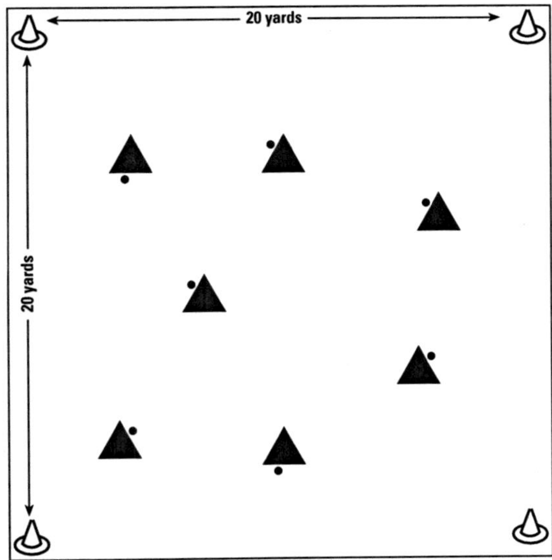

Drill #9: Sprint

Objective: To develop dribbling skills and speed while negotiating space with no defensive pressure.

Equipment Needed: One soccer ball for each player, four game markers

Description:

- Scatter players in a 20-yard-by-20-yard grid with a ball.
- The players travel through the grid until they hear the coach's whistle.
- On that signal, players dribble their balls as fast as they can out of the grid.
- Players continue dribbling as fast as they can until they hear a second whistle.
- Then, the players dribble as fast as they can back to the grid, where they continue traveling through the grid at a moderate pace.

Coaching Points: Present this drill only when players have developed sufficient ball control skills. Encourage them to push the ball away to open spaces at a distance of five to seven yards and then sprint to the ball. Kicking the ball as far as they can and sprinting after it is not the purpose of this drill.

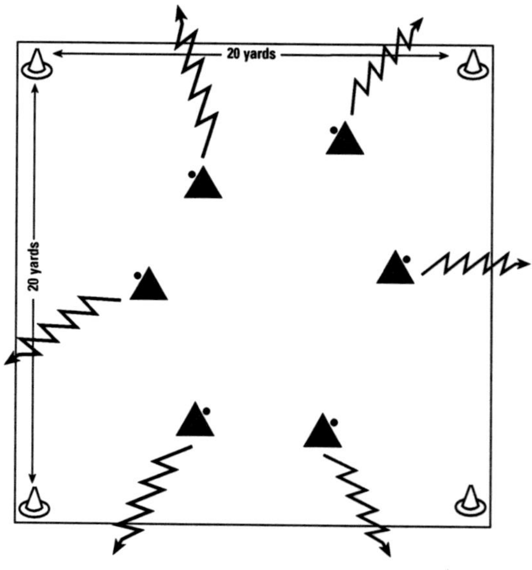

Drill #10: Circle Dribble Tag

Objective: To help develop dribbling skills while under subtle defensive pressure.

Equipment Needed: Two soccer balls and four game markers for every six players

Description:

Level 1

- Place six players in a 10-yard-by-10-yard grid.
- Four players form a circle.
- Two players, each with a ball, stand outside the circle on opposite sides.
- Designate one of these players as the tagger.
- On the coach's signal, the tagger has 30 seconds to catch the other player with a ball while both players are dribbling.
- The tagger may cut through the circle, but the player being chased may not.

Level 2

- Repeat the first six steps from Level 1.
- While the tagger is chasing the other player, teammates who have formed the circle move as a unit to shield the player being chased by the tagger.

Coaching Points: Players need to use good visual habits to know when the tagger has changed directions. Changing directions and speeds frequently will help the player being chased.

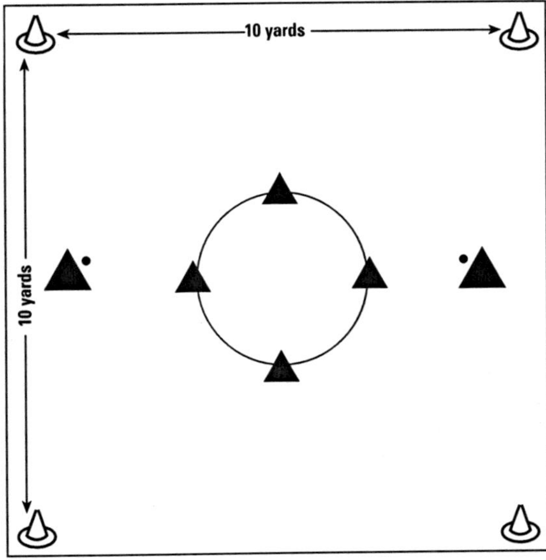

Drill #11: Shake-and-Take

Objective: To develop dribbling skills used to create space and go to goal with defensive pressure.

Equipment Needed: One soccer ball for each player, one marker for each goal, four goals

Description:

Level 1

- Place a marker 40 yards from the goal.
- A player dribbles toward the marker, executes an individual move to create space (a scissors move, for example), and then goes to the goal and shoots.

Level 2

- Place two markers 40 yards from goal about 5 yards apart.
- A defender stands on a line between the markers and tries to tackle the ball away from the attacker as he attempts to go between the markers to the goal.

Level 3

- Player A stands 40 yards from the goal.
- A defender stands 30 yards from the goal.
- The ball is passed to player A.
- When player A touches the ball, the defender may pursue him.
- Player A uses individual moves to create space to go to the goal.

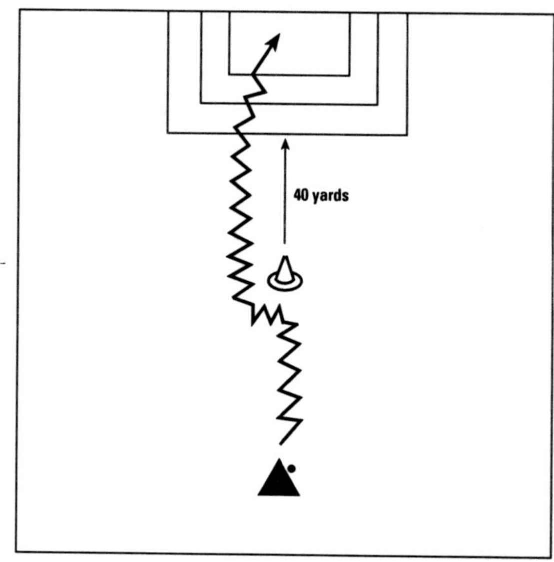

Coaching Points: All players should work to develop individual moves with imaginary pressure (the marker in Level 1) until they experience success. When their skills have improved to the point where they need more challenge, add a defender who can move only laterally (Level 2), to add subtle pressure. A defender applies game-like pressure at Level 3. Do not rush players through their progressions. Use as many goals as are available, or make temporary goals, so players have many opportunities.

White jersey player has avoided dark jersey defender and is now on

Drill #12: Sprint Challenge Drill

Objective: To develop dribbling skills and speed when confronted with game-like defensive pressure.

Equipment Needed: One soccer ball for every three players, four goals

Description:

Level 1

- Player A stands about five yards behind player B.
- The coach passes the ball forward.
- Player B must collect the ball, sprint toward the goal, and shoot before the defender can catch him.
- Variations include serving balls at various speeds, directions, and levels.

Level 2

- Repeat the first four steps from Level 1.
- Repeat the action, but add a goalkeeper to increase the defensive pressure.

Coaching Points: Encourage players to push the ball five to seven yards to maintain both speed and control. When adding a goalkeeper, restrict him by not allowing him to come off the goal line. As skills increase, add more goalkeeping pressure.

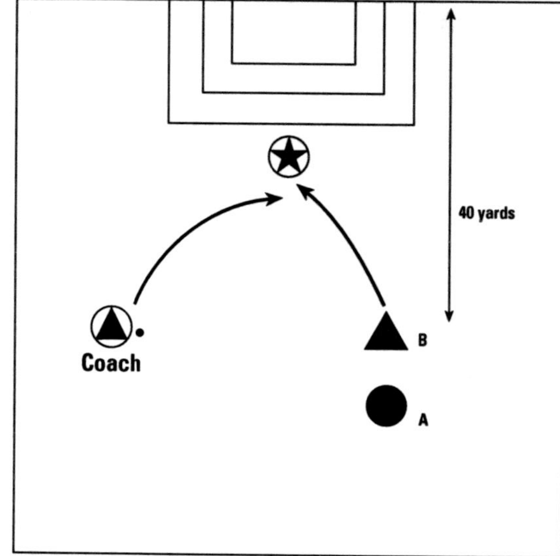

Drill #13: Partner Dribble Game

Objective: To help develop dribbling skills to create space with game-like defensive pressure.

Equipment Needed: One soccer ball and four game markers for every two players

Description:

- In a 10-yard-by-10-yard grid, one partner stands on a line with a ball, and the other partner stands on the opposite side of the square.
- Player A passes the ball to player B.
- When player B receives the ball, player A pursues him in an effort to close his space and touch the ball or force him out of the grid.
- If player A touches the ball, he earns one point.
- If player B can dribble safely to the opposite line, he earns two points.
- The first player to earn six points is the winner.
- Then, the players reverse roles.

Coaching Points: The offensive player in this drill earns more points for being successful because this is an offensive drill. Encourage the offensive player to use a variety of moves to create space.

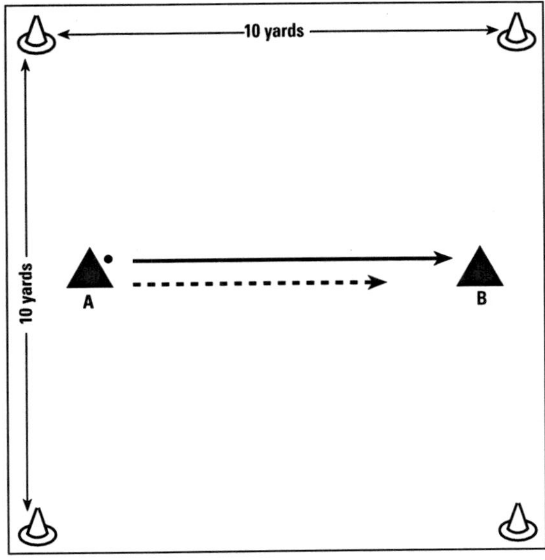

Drill #14: Force Challenge

Objective: To help develop an understanding of the application of force when passing the ball.

Equipment Needed: One soccer ball for every two players

Description:

- Players stand approximately five yards from the sideline.
- Ask players to kick the ball so that it stops on the line.
- Repeat several times.
- Request players to repeat this action from 10-, 20-, and 30-yard distances.
- Use partners to retrieve balls.

Coaching Points: Discuss the proportional relationship between leg speed and the distance the ball will travel. Encourage players to use proper kicking technique for making flat passes.

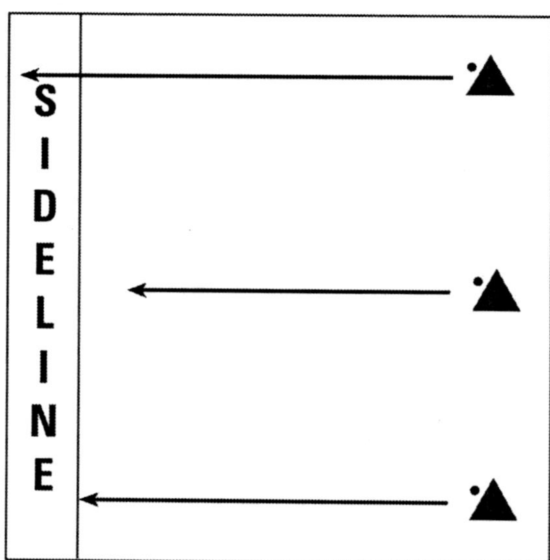

Drill #15: Partner Passing

Objective: To help develop passing accuracy and collection skills from a stationary passer to a stationary target with no defensive pressure.

Equipment Needed: One soccer ball for every two players, four game markers

Description:

Level 1

- Position players in a scattered formation in a 30-yard-by-30-yard grid.
- Partners should be about 10 yards apart.
- Players will pass to their partners, who will collect the ball and return the pass.
- Encourage players to speak aloud the sequence of collect, look, look right, and pass.
- Repeat looking left, or combining left and right, before returning the pass.

Level 2

- Repeat the first five steps from Level 1.
- Vary this activity by using three players in a triangle or several players in a circle formation.
- After a stationary player passes to a stationary target, he may run to that player's space.

Coaching Points: It is important for beginning players to stop the ball before returning it to their partners. Encourage players to relax the part of the body used for stopping the ball, as it will have a cushioning effect. By stopping the ball, players will improve the accuracy of passes because it's easier to strike a stationary ball than one in motion. Level 2 incorporates movement after the pass, which will help to establish the philosophy that the passer should continue to be a player instead of becoming a spectator after passing. Later, this movement will lead to executing wall passes.

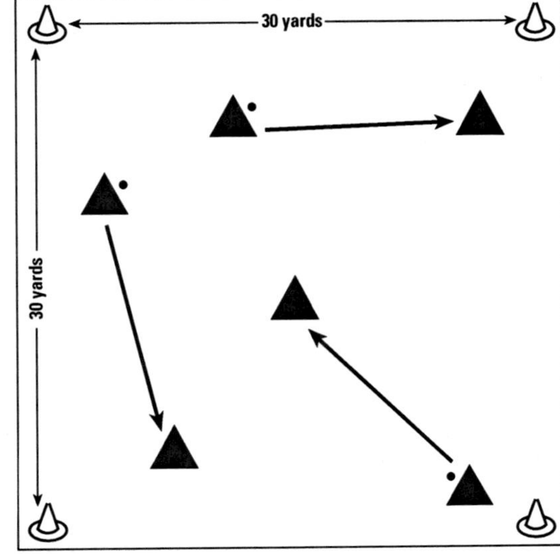

Drill #16: Thread-the-Needle

Objective: To help improve passing accuracy and collection skills from a stationary passer to a stationary target with no defensive pressure.

Equipment Needed: One soccer ball and two game markers for every two players

Description:

- Scatter partners with two cones between them.
- Place cones initially about three or four yards apart.
- Instruct players to pass to each other by having the ball go between the markers.
- Have some fun with this drill by making it a game.
- On the coach's signal, players begin passing.
- After each successful pass, they take one step backward.
- If the ball does not go between the markers, players must return to the starting point and begin again.
- After two minutes, stop and see how far apart partners are.

Coaching Points: Begin this drill with partners approximately 10 yards apart. As the skill level of the players improves, increase the distance between the players and decrease the distance between the markers. To assess player performance, count how many times the players are able to pass the ball between the markers in 20 attempts. Insure that players are collecting and bringing the ball to a stop before returning the pass.

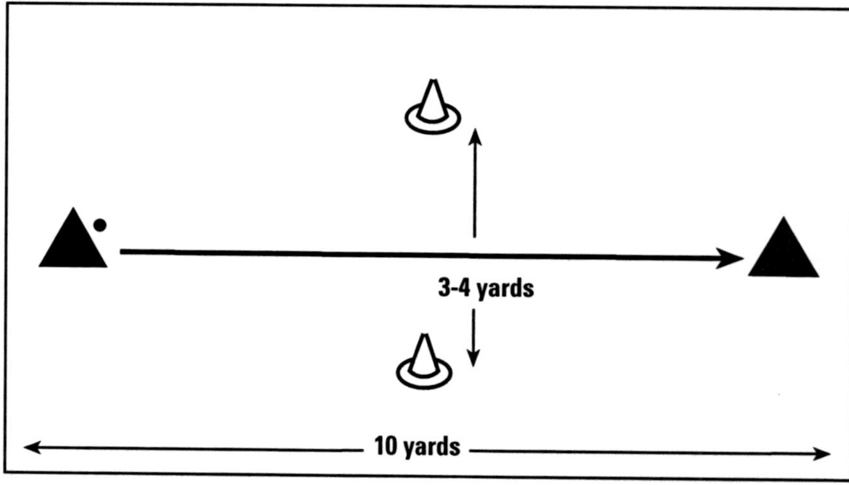

Drill #17: Tunnel Connection

Objective: To help improve passing accuracy and collection skills from a stationary passer to a stationary target with no defensive pressure.

Equipment Needed: One soccer ball for every three players

Description:

- Three players stand in a line approximately 10 yards apart.
- Player A passes the ball through player B's legs to player C.
- Player B then switches with player A.
- Player C passes through player A's legs to player B and then switches with player A.
- Repeat action several times.

Coaching Points: Encourage players to collect and wait for their partners to get to their positions before passing. Without patience, spacing becomes a problem with this drill. If necessary, place markers at 10-yard intervals to help players with spacing.

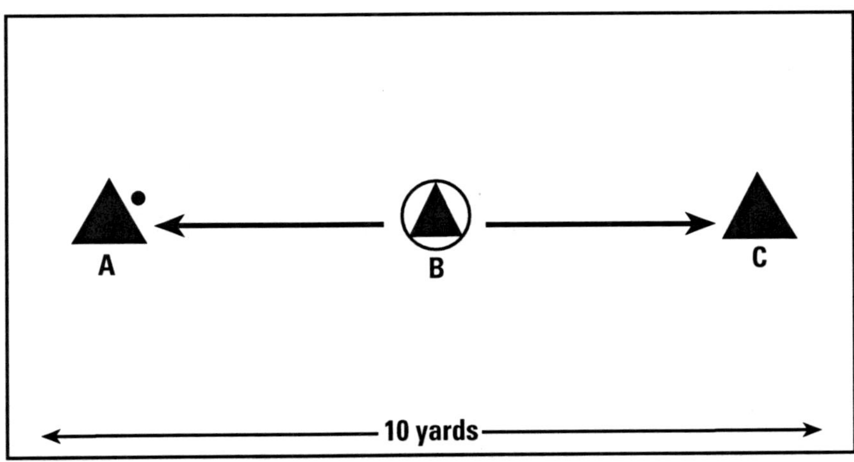

Drill #18: Good-bye

Objective: To help develop passing accuracy and collection skills from a stationary passer to a stationary target and initiate movement after the pass with no defensive pressure.

Equipment Needed: One soccer ball and four game markers for every three players

Description:

Level 1

- Position three players in a 10-yard-by-10-yard grid so that they each occupy a corner of the grid.
- Player A will pass to player B, then say good-bye, and travel to the unoccupied corner of the grid.
- Player B then passes to player C, says good-bye, and travels to the corner vacated by player A.
- Repeat this action several times.

Level 2

- After players feel comfortable with the spacing provided by the 10-yard grid, remove the game markers.
- Request that all players travel in threes, repeating the movement in general space.

Coaching Points: Encourage players to deliver crisp, flat passes that will be easy to collect. Players should pass and move quickly to the open space. Reinforce this repeated action of pass and move in scrimmages and games. At Level 2, encourage players to move through open spaces as they negotiate other players and maintain 10-yard spacing.

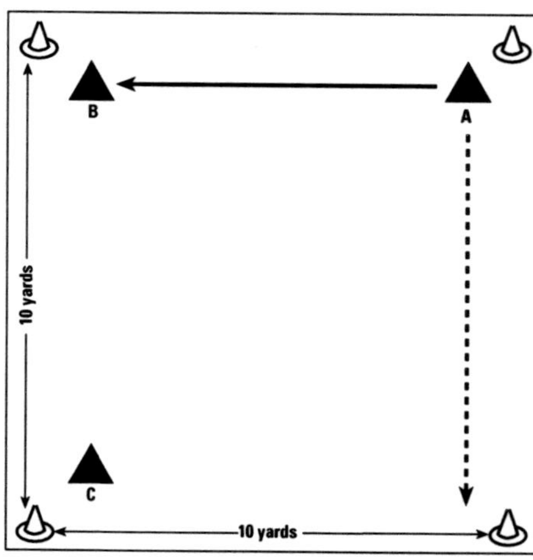

Drill #19: Circle Collection

Objective: To help develop passing accuracy and collection skills from stationary passer to moving target with no defensive pressure.

Equipment Needed: Soccer balls for every player

Description:

- Six players form a circle.
- Each player has a ball.
- Three players are in constant motion inside the circle.
- As an inside player makes eye contact with a player on the circle, the ball is passed to him.
- He returns the pass to the player who passed it and moves to another space to collect another pass.
- Players forming the circle exchange places every one to two minutes.

Coaching Points: Caution moving players inside the circle to pass through open spaces. Players on the inside should collect, look, and make a good decision concerning their next pass.

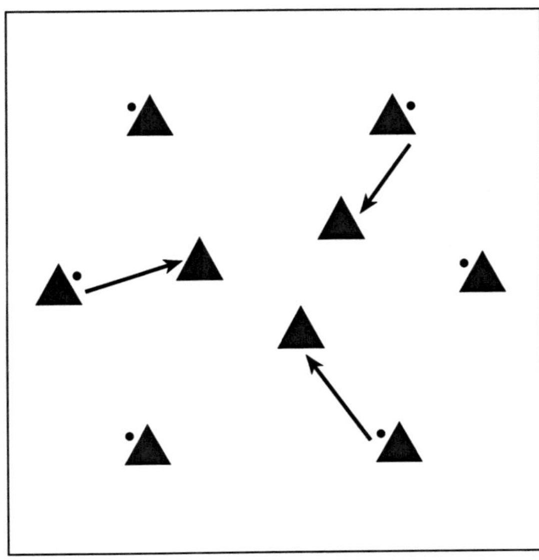

Drill #20: Hello

Objective: To help develop passing accuracy and collection skills from a stationary passer to a moving target with no defensive pressure.

Equipment Needed: One soccer ball and four game markers for every three players

Description:

Level 1

- Position three players, each in a corner of a 10-yard-by-10-yard grid.
- Player C, closest to the unoccupied corner and not in possession of the ball, will move to the unoccupied corner and say the word "hello."
- Player A, with the ball, passes to player C.
- Player B then moves to the space vacated by player C to receive a pass from player C.

Level 2

- As players become comfortable with spacing, remove game markers. Have several groups of players moving in one large grid repeating Level 1 action.

Coaching Points: Coaches should encourage players moving to space to give an oral reminder to the passer. In this drill, they should be saying "hello." For the sake of consistency, coaches may want their players to say the word "space." Moving players should wait until the passer has controlled the ball and has made eye contact before initiating any movement. Discuss with players how delivering a soft pass to a player coming toward the ball will aid the collection process.

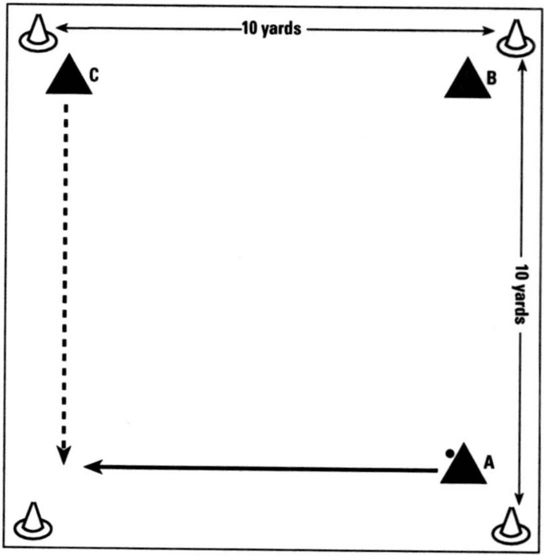

Drill #21: Spaceman

Objective: To help develop passing accuracy and collection skills from a stationary passer to a moving target with no defensive pressure.

Equipment Needed: One soccer ball and three game markers for every two players

Description:

Level 1

- Position two players in a triangle identified by markers placed 10 yards apart.
- Each player occupies a corner of the triangle.
- The player without the ball runs to the unoccupied corner of the triangle and says loudly the word "space."
- The player with the ball passes it to the moving player.
- The player who passed the ball moves to the unoccupied corner to receive a return pass.
- Repeat this action several times.

Level 2

- Remove game markers. Have partners travel through general space using a triangular pattern with 10-yard spacing.

Coaching Points: Encourage the player moving to open space to make eye contact with the passer to insure that the passer has the ball in control to make a pass. Instruct the passer to lead the player moving to space by passing the ball slightly ahead of him so he doesn't have to break stride to collect the ball. Timing runs and communicating well are important to the success of this drill.

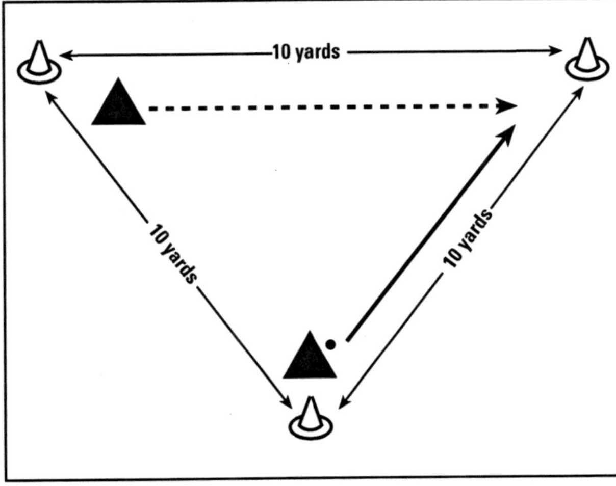

Drill #22: Diagonal Passing

Objective: To develop passing accuracy and collection skills from a moving passer to a stationary target with no defensive pressure.

Equipment Needed: One soccer ball and four game markers for every three players

Description:

Level 1

- Position three players in a 10-yard-by-10-yard grid so that each occupies a corner space.
- Player A dribbles to the unoccupied corner and passes diagonally to player B.
- Player B dribbles to the corner vacated by player A and passes to player C.
- Repeat action several times.

Level 2

- Remove the game markers.
- Have players move through general space repeating this action.

Coaching Points: A player must use a controlled dribble to keep the ball in the grid. He must turn his nonkicking foot slightly toward the target before passing. This adjustment will allow the hips to rotate and the kicking foot to swing outside of the ball before impact. At Level 2, encourage players to maintain 10-yard spacing and avoid closed spaces.

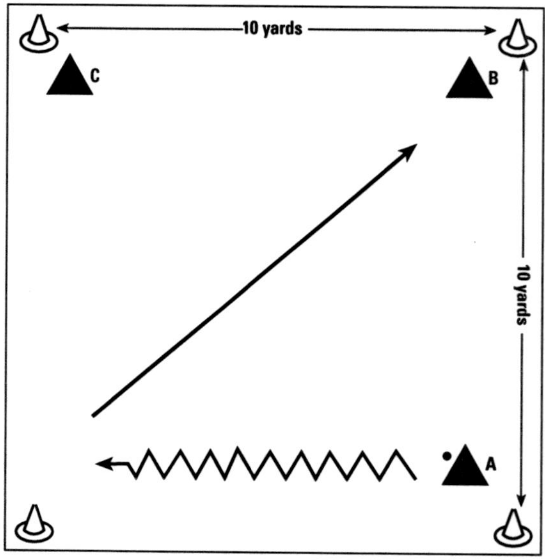

Drill #23: Return-to-Sender

Objective: To help develop passing accuracy and collection skills from a moving passer to a stationary target with no defensive pressure.

Equipment Needed: One soccer ball for every two players, four game markers, two sets of jerseys—one jersey for each player

Description:

- Scatter players in a 30-yard-by-30-yard grid.
- Divide the group into two equal teams with different jerseys.
- The players with striped jerseys, each with a ball, move freely in a grid.
- As they approach a stationary player with a solid-colored jersey, they will pass to him, collect the return pass, and then move through space, finding another solid-colored team member to whom they will pass.
- Repeat for one minute, making as many passes as possible to different players.
- Then, reverse roles.
- Vary this drill by delivering passes at different levels.

Coaching Points: This drill will go more smoothly for beginning players if the stationary players collect the ball with their hands and then roll it to the passer, who should be moving to a new space. As the players become more skillful, require them to collect with various body parts or execute one-touch passes.

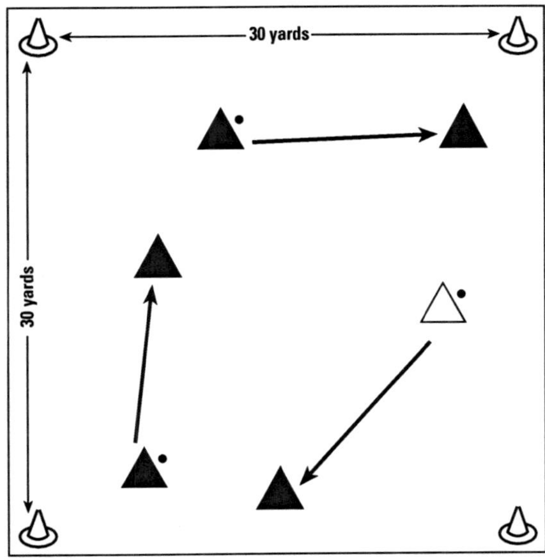

Drill #24: Four-Corner Passing

Objective: To help develop passing accuracy and collection skills from a moving passer to a moving target with no defensive pressure.

Equipment Needed: One soccer ball and four game markers for every five players

Description:

- Position players in a 10-yard-by-10-yard grid so that players occupy the corners of the grid.
- Player E will be outside the grid beside player A, ready to occupy that space when player A leaves.
- Player A moves toward, and passes to, player B, who begins to move when player A reaches the halfway point between them.
- After passing to player B, player A continues to move and occupies player B's original space.
- Player B collects on the move and passes to player C, who begins to move when player B reaches the halfway point between them.
- Players continue this action of collecting while moving, passing to the next player, and then occupying his corner of the grid.
- As passing skills improve, challenge players by counting how many times they can pass the ball around the entire grid in two minutes.

Coaching Points: Passers should make eye contact with players they are passing to and should lead them with a pass that they can easily collect. You may use more players in this drill by positioning them by the corners outside the grid. As a player completes the pass, he would then go to the end of the line instead of standing by the marker.

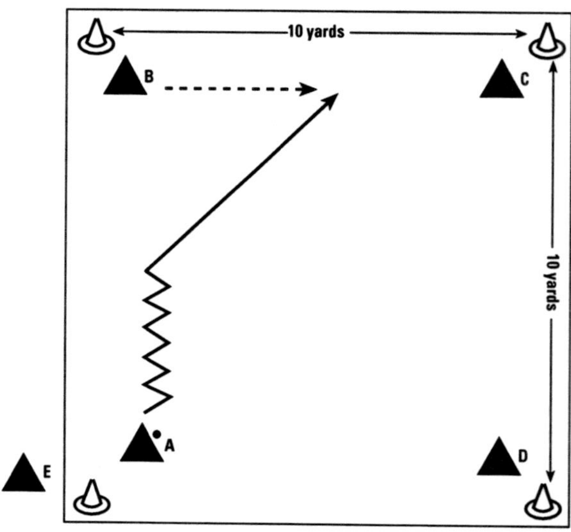

Drill #25: Pass-Dribble-Pass

Objective: To help develop passing accuracy and collection skills from a moving passer to a moving target with no defensive pressure.

Equipment Needed: One soccer ball and four game markers for every two players

Description:

Level 1

- Position two players in a 15-yard-by-15-yard grid.
- Player A will pass to player B, who dribbles into open space and then turns and passes back to player A, who has moved to a new space behind him.
- Repeat this action.

Level 2

- Remove game markers.
- Players repeat action moving in general space.

Coaching Points: This drill requires players to pass the ball in a backward direction. Players taking space behind another player should communicate that they are in an open space by saying the word "drop." Players passing in a backward direction should begin developing the use of the heel to pass and changing the position of their body in relation to the ball as demonstrated on the stepover move. At Level 2, encourage partners to communicate. With all partner groups moving in general space, partners sometimes become separated without this communication.

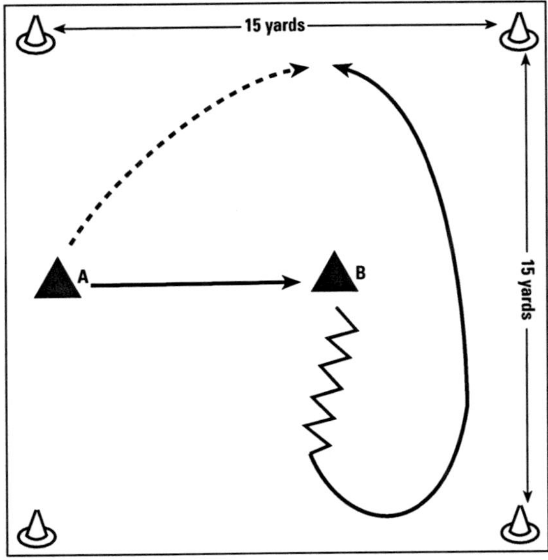

Drill #26: First-Touch

Objective: To help develop passing accuracy from a moving passer to a moving target with no defensive pressure.

Equipment Needed: One soccer ball for every two players and four game markers

Description:

- Scatter players in pairs in a 20-yard-by-20-yard grid.
- Each set of partners has a ball.
- On the coach's signal, the players begin to move through the grid.
- The players with the ball pass to their partners, who must pass back on the first touch.
- Partners continue moving using only one-touch passing.

Coaching Points: Players must use good visual habits in negotiating space to avoid other players. Initially partners should move with spacing no more than three or four yards apart. As they become more proficient with their one-touch passing, they can separate by greater distances.

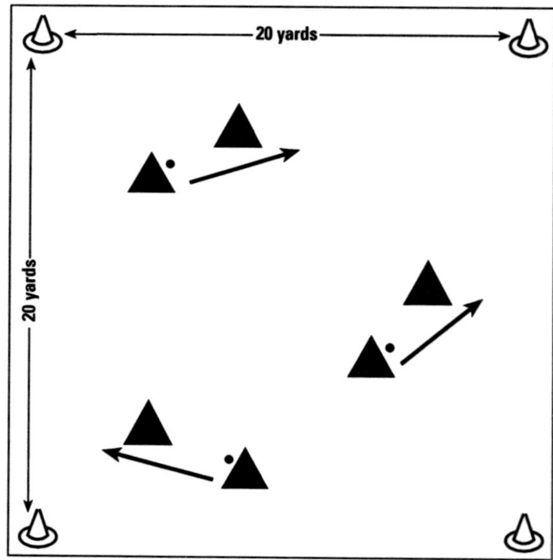

Drill #27: Star

Objective: To help develop passing and collection skills with subtle defensive pressure.

Equipment Needed: One soccer ball for every six players

Description:

- Position five players to form points of a star.
- Place one defender in the middle of the star.
- Challenge players to make as many consecutive passes as possible without losing control or allowing the defender to touch the ball.
- Do not allow players to pass the ball to players beside them.

Coaching Points: This is a five-versus-one drill. The offensive players have a big advantage. Beginning players need this advantage to collect, look, and make good decisions with the ball.

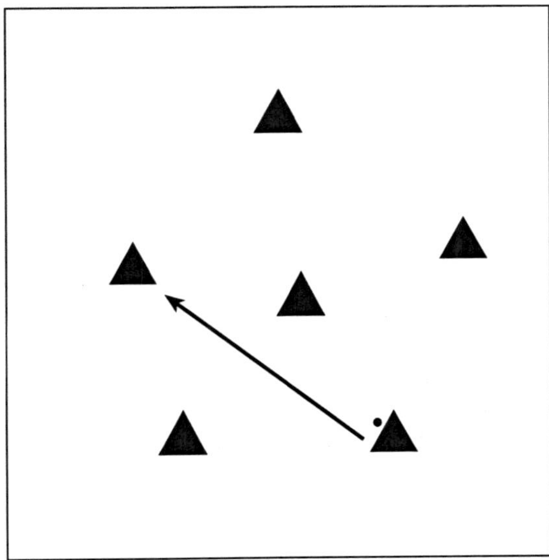

Drill #28: Monkey-in-the-Middle

Objective: To help develop passing and collection skills with subtle pressure, movement without the ball, and decision-making ability concerning the use of open versus closed space.

Equipment Needed: One soccer ball and four game markers for every four players

Description:

- Players occupy spaces by three of the markers.
- A fourth player is in the middle and is affectionately referred to as the "monkey."
- The perimeter players are playing a three-versus-one keep-away game.
- Players are not allowed to pass the ball across the middle of the square.
- This rule forces the perimeter players to move constantly to support positions so the player with the ball always has two passing lanes from which to choose.
- For example, if the ball were by cone A, players would support in spaces by cone B and cone D.
- If the player in the middle, the defender, closes the space between A and B, then the pass is made to the player at cone D.
- Then, support positioning would go to cone A and cone C.
- Since a player already occupies cone A, the player who was at cone B would move to cone C to support.
- It is impossible for the defender to close both passing lanes.
- The defender earns his way out of the middle by touching the ball or forcing an error in passing or collecting.

Coaching Points: Perimeter players must collect, look, and make a decision about passing choices. Perimeter players must communicate with each other concerning space. Variations might include limiting touches on the ball, using diagonal runs to space, or allowing dribbling to space.

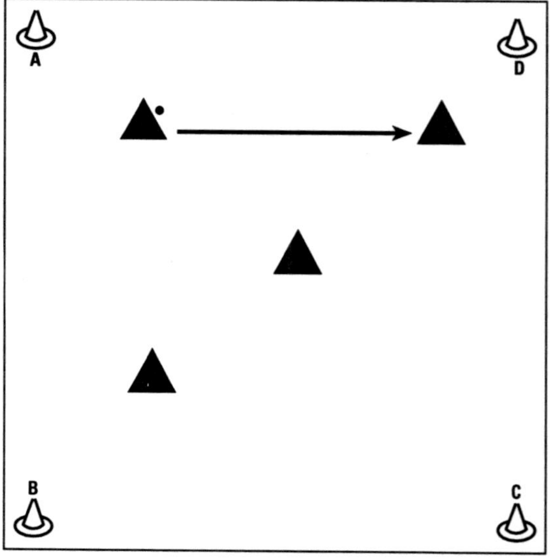

Drill #29: Cone

Objective: To help develop passing and collection skills with game-like defensive pressure.

Equipment Needed: One soccer ball and five game markers for every six players

Description:

- Position a player on each side of a 15-yard-by-15-yard grid.
- One player has a ball.
- Place a game marker in the center of the grid.
- Two players are inside the grid.
- One is an offensive player; the other is a defensive player.
- The offensive player must run around the cone and sprint toward the player with the ball.
- The player with the ball passes to the offensive player if he is in an open space.
- If the defender closes his space, the passer passes instead to another player on the grid.
- The offensive player repeats, going around the cone toward the new player with the ball.
- The offensive player collects and returns the ball each time to the passer, who then passes to another player on the perimeter of the grid.

Coaching Points: Challenge players to count how many times the offensive player receives a pass in one minute. Passers must give the offensive players soft passes to collect. Defensive players work hard to close the space between the offensive player and the passer. Vary the degree of difficulty for collection by serving balls at various speeds and levels to challenge more advanced players.

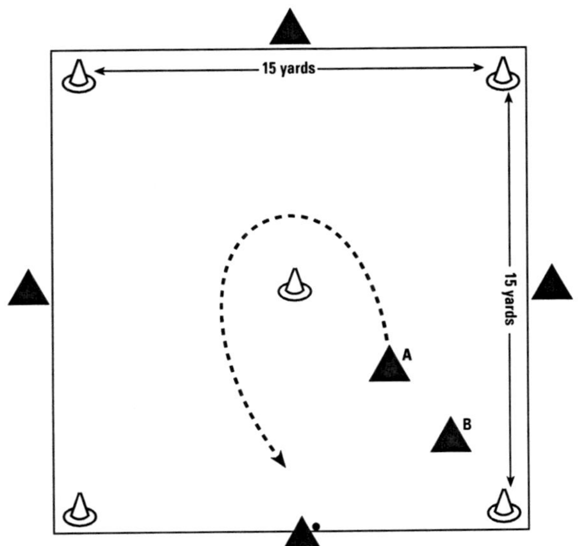

Drill #30: Check-Out/Check-In

Objective: To help develop passing and collection skills with game-like defensive pressure.

Equipment Needed: One soccer ball and four game markers for every six players

Description:

- Position a player on each side of a 15-yard-by-15-yard grid.
- One player has the ball.
- Two players are inside the grid.
- Player A runs away (checks out) from the ball, changes direction, and then sprints toward the ball (checks in) to receive a pass.
- If the defender (player B) closes the space, the passer plays the ball to another player on the grid.
- If the offensive player collects the pass, he should shield the ball for 5 to 10 seconds before returning a pass.
- Challenge players to count how many consecutive passes the offensive player receives in one minute without the defensive player touching the ball.

Coaching Points: Offensive players should move away from the ball at a moderate rate of speed. After changing directions, offensive players should accelerate toward the ball. Changing speeds makes denying space more difficult for the defender.

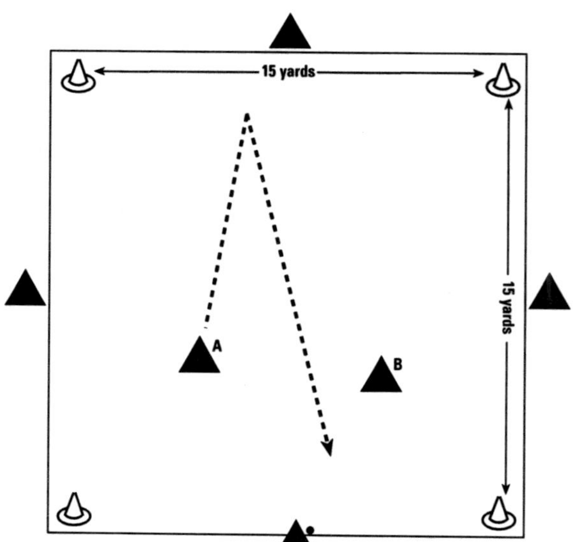

Drill #31: Three-Versus-Two

Objective: To help develop decision-making abilities concerning passing choices with game-like defensive pressure.

Equipment Needed: One soccer ball and two goals for every seven players

Description:

- Place two goals approximately 30 yards apart.
- Position players so that three offensive players are in the middle of the field ready to score against two defenders.
- Position two defenders at each end of the field.
- On the coach's signal, the three offensive players pass the ball until they get close enough to the goal to shoot.
- The player who takes the shot then joins the two defenders to try to score against the two defenders at the opposite end of the field.
- If a defender steals a pass, that defending group goes on the attack with the person from whom they stole the pass.

Coaching Points: Offensive players have a numbers advantage, so there should always be an open player. Encourage players to make switching and overlapping runs to create space. Challenge players by allowing them no more than two touches on the ball.

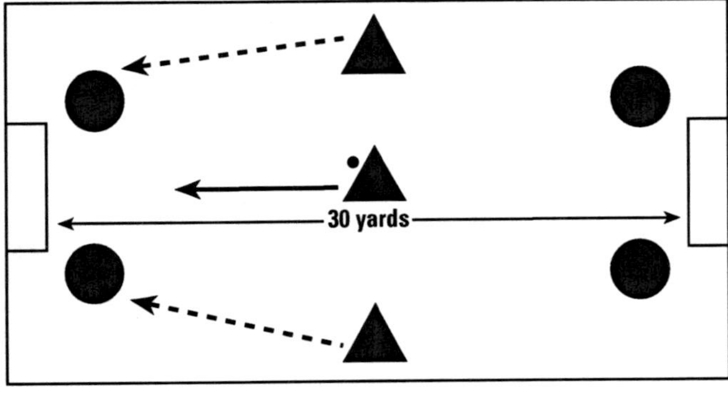

Drill #32: One-Versus-One

Objective: To help develop decision-making abilities concerning passing choices with game-like defensive pressure.

Equipment Needed: One soccer ball, one jersey for defender, two jerseys (different color from the defender's jersey) for neutral players, and four game markers for every four players

Description:

Level 1

- Position four players in a 15-yard-by-15-yard grid—one offensive, one defensive, and two neutral players.
- The offensive player passes to one of the neutral players and then moves to open space to receive a return pass.
- Players try to connect as many consecutive passes as possible.
- If the defender gains possession, he becomes the offensive player.
- After one minute of possession, switch roles.

Level 2

- Use only one neutral player.
- Apply a two-touch limit.

Coaching Points: Players must quickly change speeds and directions to create the spaces for passes. Variations of this drill include adding players to make two-versus-two or three-versus-three. Add goals to encourage finishing skills. Neutral players may not be defended.

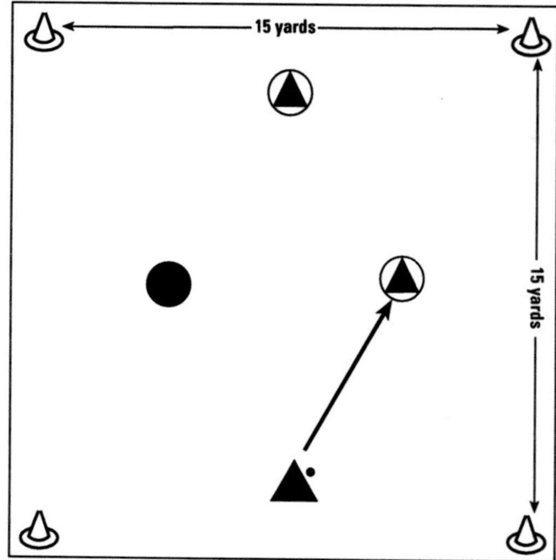

Drill #33: Partner Stationary Shooting

Objective: To help develop proper kicking techniques for shooting a stationary ball from a stationary position with no defensive pressure.

Equipment Needed: One soccer ball for every two players

Description:

- In a scattered formation, position partners so that they are 10 to 15 yards apart.
- The partner without the ball should assume a goalkeeper's stance, with hands in a ready position.
- The other partner will approach the stationary ball and shoot, trying to hit his partner.

Coaching Points: Beginning players are sometimes not accurate while shooting. Therefore, it may be necessary to increase the number of goalkeepers a player is shooting toward. For example, space three goalkeepers in ready positions about 10 feet apart and have the shooter aim for the middle one. Players will spend less time chasing errant kicks. Reinforce a philosophy of accuracy over power during this drill. To help improve accuracy, encourage players to watch their foot strike the ball. Emphasize the use of the instep position of the foot as opposed to the toes.

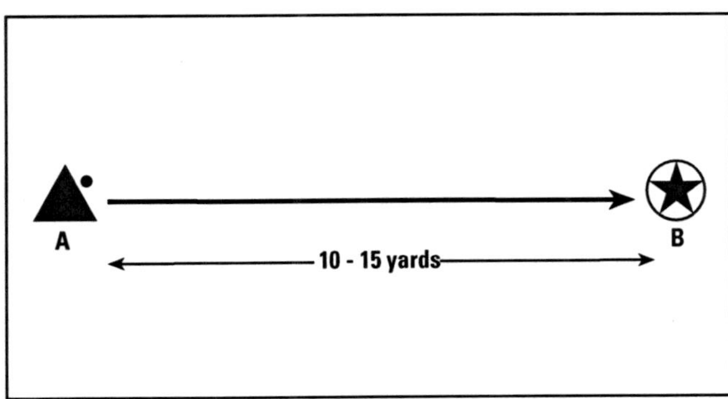

Drill #34: Three-Player Shooting

Objective: To help develop proper kicking techniques for shooting a stationary ball from a stationary position with no defensive pressure.

Equipment *Needed*: One soccer ball for every three players

Description:

- Position three players in a line approximately 10 yards apart.
- Player A shoots the ball at player B, who is in a goalkeeper's stance.
- Player B collects the ball and rolls it to player C.
- Player C stops the ball and then shoots at player B.
- After several shots, rotate players.

Coaching Points: Emphasize striking a stationary ball with the instep of the foot. Promote the philosophy of shooting accuracy over shooting power. As the players become more competent with shooting skills, increase the distance between players.

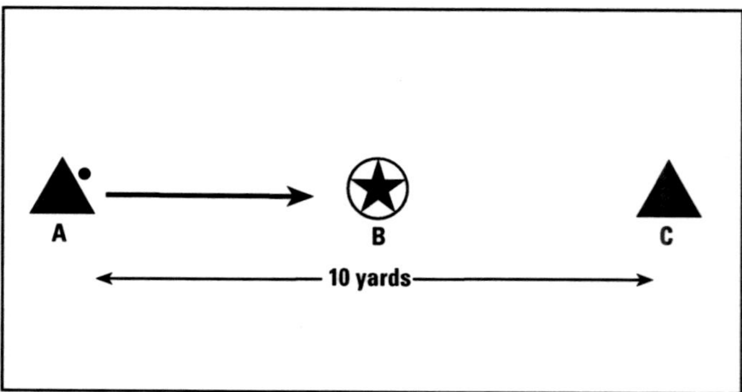

Drill #35: Open-Corner

Objective: To help develop shooting accuracy from a stationary position with a stationary ball and no defensive pressure.

Equipment Needed: One soccer ball per player, four goals

Description:

Level 1

- Place several balls in a row approximately 12 to 15 yards from the goal.
- Players will shoot the balls into the unoccupied goal.

Level 2

- Repeat the first two steps from Level 1.
- Place a goalkeeper slightly to one side of the goal.
- Challenge the players to shoot to the unoccupied corner.

Coaching Points: Once players have developed a proper kicking technique, they should develop an understanding of placement. Encourage players, during Level 1 of this drill, to shoot for the corners. When you add a goalkeeper at Level 2, restrict the keeper's movement by using game markers to establish how far he may move on the goal line. Do this drill as part of small-group work using portable or temporary goals, or as part of station work as players are arriving to practice. Using the drill in large-group work will result in too much standing.

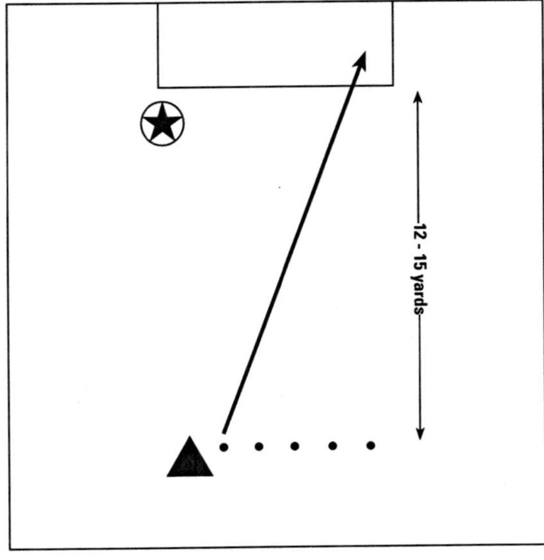

Drill #36: Run-and-Shoot

Objective: To help develop proper kicking technique when the shooter is in motion, the ball is stationary, and no defensive pressure exists.

Equipment Needed: Four soccer balls, one goal, four game markers for every four players

Description:

Level 1

- Place several balls in a row in a 15-yard-by-15-yard grid.
- The shooter runs around one of the markers and shoots the ball in the goal.
- Repeat several times with the shooter running around a different marker each time.

Level 2

- Repeat the first three steps from Level 1.
- Place a goalkeeper outside each goal post.
- As the shooter makes the turn around the marker, signal one of the goalkeepers to step in one corner of the goal.
- The shooter must shoot to the unoccupied corner.

Coaching Points: Requiring the shooter to run around different markers will vary the angle of the kick. During Level 2 action, goalkeepers must stay inside the goal on their side, which forces shooters to look up to determine where to place the ball. During Level 1, one player shoots, two retrieve balls, and one player resets balls for next shooter. During Level 2, one player shoots, two act as goalkeepers, and the other retrieves balls. Coaches may want to use this drill as a station for circuit training. If you use this drill as a large-group activity, use regular and temporary goals. Emphasize shooting low at the temporary goals and high at the regular goals.

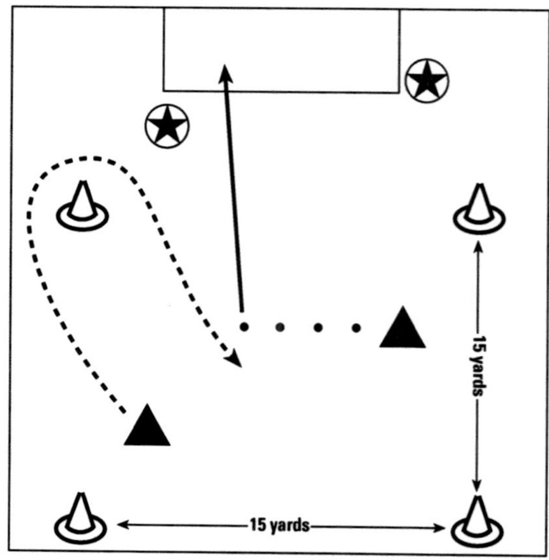

Drill #37: Pass-and-Shoot

Objective: To help develop proper kicking technique by a stationary player shooting a moving ball with no defensive pressure.

Equipment Needed: One soccer ball and two goals for every four players

Description:

- Place two goals 30 yards apart.
- Position players as shown in the diagram.
- Player B serves to player C, who shoots at goalkeeper D.
- Goalkeeper D passes to player C. Player C passes to player B, who shoots at goalkeeper A.
- Repeat several times and reverse roles.

Coaching Points: Keep several balls in the goals for goalkeepers to pass, to keep the drill fast-paced. Encourage one-touch shooting to the corners of the goals.

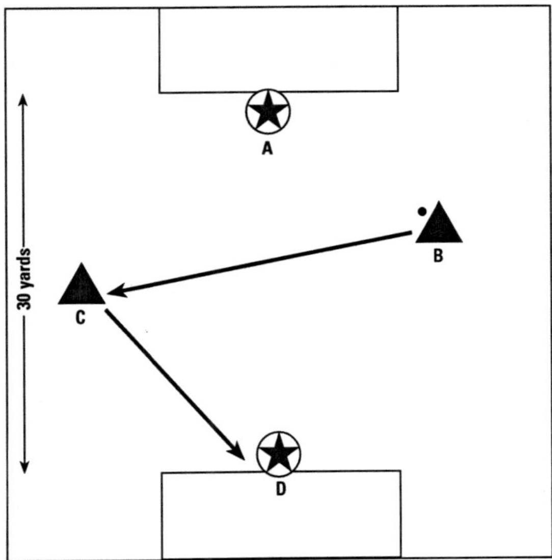

Drill #38: Over-the-Goal Shooting

Objective: To help develop proper kicking technique for shooting a moving ball at various levels by a stationary player with no defensive pressure.

Equipment Needed: Three soccer balls and one goal for every three players

Description:

- Position three players by placing one behind, one in front, and one in the goal.
- Player A serves the ball over the goal to player C, who is approximately 15 to 20 yards from goal.
- Player C shoots at goalkeeper B.
- Player A will serve three balls; then players change roles.

Coaching Points: Moving balls served at various levels are very challenging for beginning players. Allow the shooter at least one touch to settle the ball a little before shooting. As skills improve, request that the players shoot the ball toward the goal on the first touch. Emphasize striking the middle or top half of the ball on its descent. This technique will help to keep the shot low.

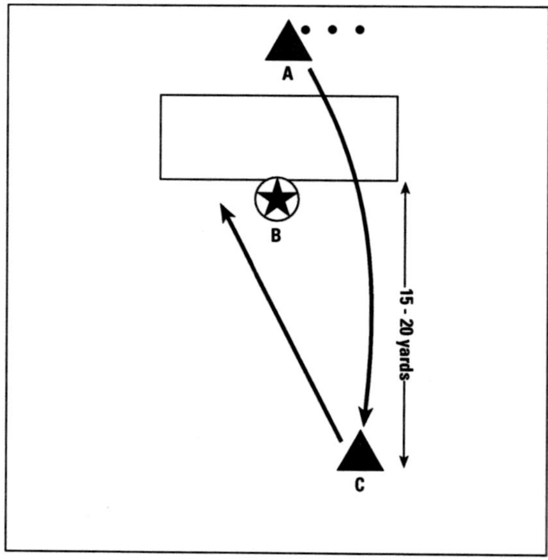

Drill #39: Alternating Shooting

Objective: To help develop proper kicking technique for shooting a moving ball by a moving player with no defensive pressure.

Equipment Needed: Four soccer balls and one set of goals for every four players

Description:

- Place two goals 30 yards apart.
- Position two players in the center of the field.
- Player B will serve balls alternately right and left.
- Player A must go after the ball and shoot at the goal that is in the direction the ball is traveling.
- Player A then returns to shoot in the opposite direction.

Coaching Points: Moving players, shooting moving balls, must gather a lot of information in a short time. They must compute the direction, speed, and level of the ball. Moving players must also compute their speed, their angle to the ball, their level relative to the ball, the distance from the goal, and the position of the goalkeeper. For these reasons, the moving-ball/moving-player phase should be last in the shooting progression.

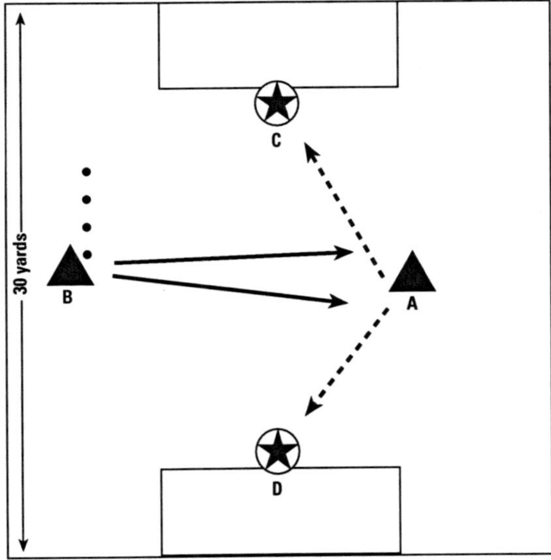

Drill #40: Spin-Turn Shooting

Objective: To help develop creating space for shooting a moving ball by a moving player with no defensive pressure.

Equipment Needed: One soccer ball and one goal for every two players

Description:

- Position players in the offensive third of the field.
- Player A, in the penalty box, makes a horizontal run and then checks back for the ball.
- Player B will pass to player A, who returns the ball to player B with a one-touch pass.
- After returning the pass, player A spins to the outside to create space for player B to return pass for a shot.

Coaching Points: Players should pivot on the inside foot (the foot closest to the goal) when spinning to the outside. Players should alternate between spinning wide, to create enough space for a pass, and spinning close to the defender to get behind him.

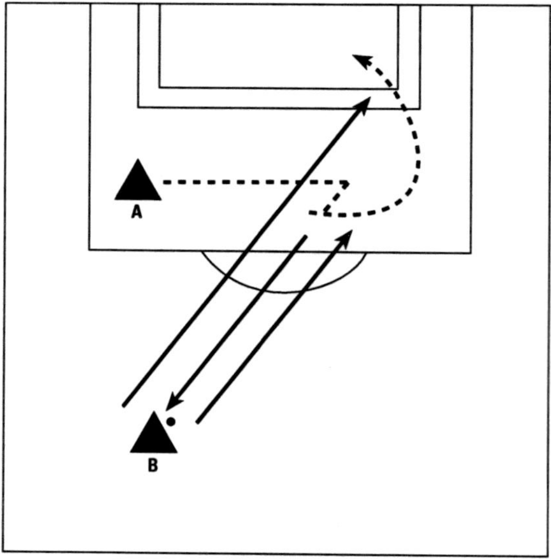

Drill #41: Circle-Pin

Objective: To help develop shooting accuracy with subtle defensive pressure.

Equipment Needed: One soccer ball, four game markers, one bowling pin for every six players

Description:

- Position five players to form a circle.
- Inside the circle, place four game markers to form a square.
- Place a bowling pin inside the square.
- Designate a sixth player to defend the pin without going inside the square.
- Players will pass the ball until a good shot opportunity is available.
- If a player shoots and knocks down the pin, he replaces the defender.

Coaching Points: Emphasize to players that they should pass the ball quickly to make the defender change directions, thus creating space for a good shot.

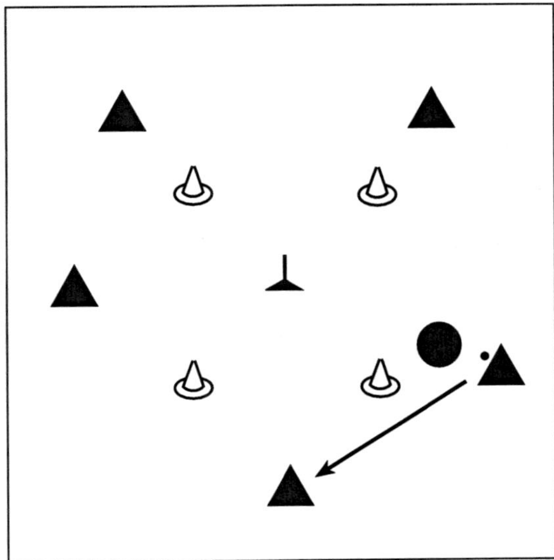

Drill #42: Three-Versus-One Shooting

Objective: To help develop proper kicking techniques for a moving player shooting a moving ball, with subtle defensive pressure.

Equipment Needed: One soccer ball and one goal for every four players, one jersey for every goalkeeper

Description:

Level 1

- Position players approximately 30 yards from the goal.
- Offensive players A, B, and C connect a series of passes until one of them takes a shot.
- One defender provides subtle pressure.

Level 2

- Repeat the first two steps from Level 1.
- Add a goalkeeper to provide more defensive pressure.

Coaching Points: Each offensive player must touch the ball before a shot may be taken. Encourage creative movement, like switching and overlapping runs. To encourage goal scoring, give the offensive players a numbers advantage such as this drill provides.

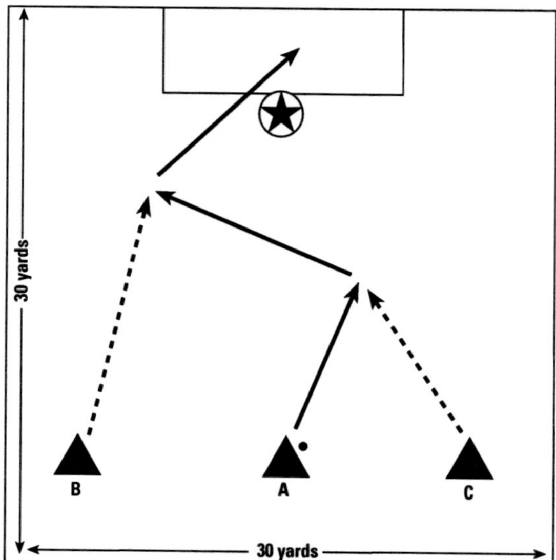

Drill #43: Wall Pass Shooting

Objective: To help develop abilities to create space for shooting with game-like defensive pressure.

Equipment Needed: One soccer ball and one goal for every four players

Description:

Level 1

- Position players in the defensive third of the field.
- Player A is the offensive player; player B is the defender.
- Player A must pass to player 1 or player 2, as a target, then move to open space for a return pass and shot.
- Player B should defend aggressively.

Level 2

- The ball is served to player A.
- Player A must collect and take on the defender with individual moves to create space for a shot or use players 1 and 2 for wall passes.

Level 3

- Repeat the first two steps from Level 2.
- Add a goalkeeper to increase defensive pressure.

Coaching Points: Encourage players to change speeds, using quick bursts to create spaces for shots.

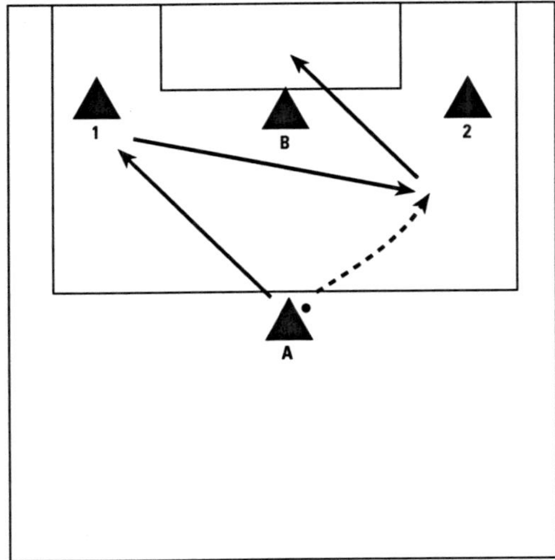

Drill #44: Line

Objective: To help develop passing accuracy and collection skills from a moving player to a stationary target with no defensive pressure.

Equipment Needed: One soccer ball and two game markers for every three players

Description:

- Place two game markers three to four yards apart.
- Position three players in a line.
- Player B passes to player A, who collects, dribbles toward player C, and passes to player C.
- Player C collects and dribbles toward player B, who took the place of player A.
- Repeat this action several times.

Coaching Points: This fast-paced drill will provide lots of touches on the ball. Encourage players to make collection as easy as possible by delivering flat, soft passes.

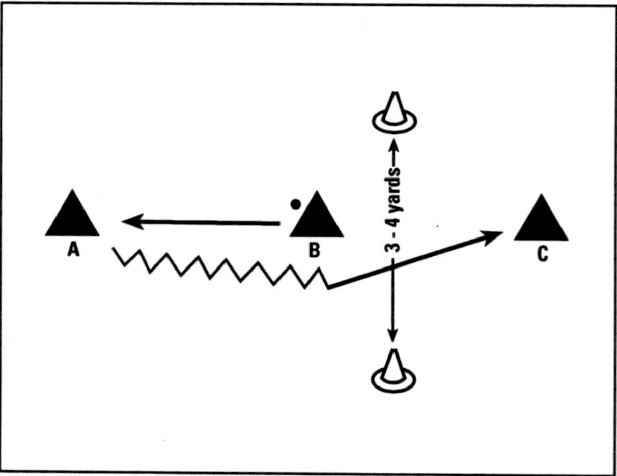

Drill #45: Pendulum

Objective: To help develop passing accuracy and collection skills from a stationary passer to a moving target with no defensive pressure.

Equipment Needed: Two soccer balls and four game markers for every three players

Description:

- Position three players in a 10-yard-by-10-yard grid.
- Two players will each have a ball on one side of the grid.
- A third player will be on the opposite side.
- The player without the ball will move to the unoccupied corner.
- As he moves, the player on that side will pass the ball.
- The moving player will collect the ball and return it to the player who passed it to him, and then run to the corner he just left to receive a pass from the other player.
- Continue this back-and-forth movement.
- After one minute, switch roles.
- After skills improve, play the pendulum game by counting how many passes a player can make in one minute.

Coaching Points: Encourage players to make flat passes with the correct amount of force that will be easy to collect. Discuss how the speed of the player will affect how far the passer must lead the pass.

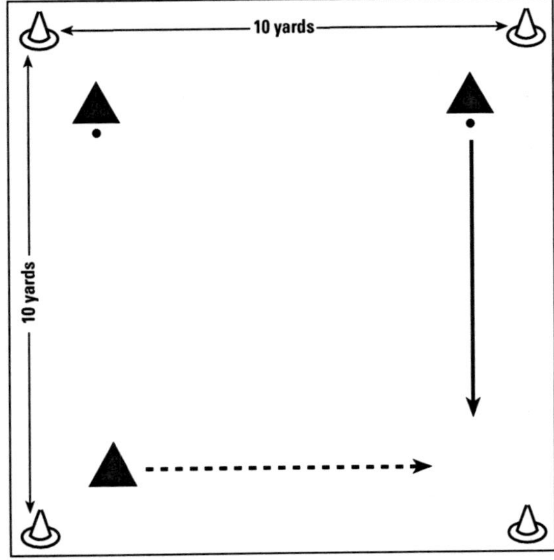

Drill #46: Invisible Man

Objective: To help develop passing and collection skills with subtle defensive pressure.

Equipment Needed: One soccer ball and four game markers for every three players

Description:

- Position three players in a 10-yard-by-10-yard grid.
- Players should be in a straight line with players B and C looking in the direction of player A.
- Player B can move laterally, but not forward or backward.
- Player C moves either right or left to receive a pass from player A.
- Player B then faces player C, and players repeat the action.
- After several chances, change defenders.

Coaching Points: The addition of the defender will add a subtle pressure to the passer because it will affect his vision. In fact, if player C does not move into open space, he is practically invisible to player A.

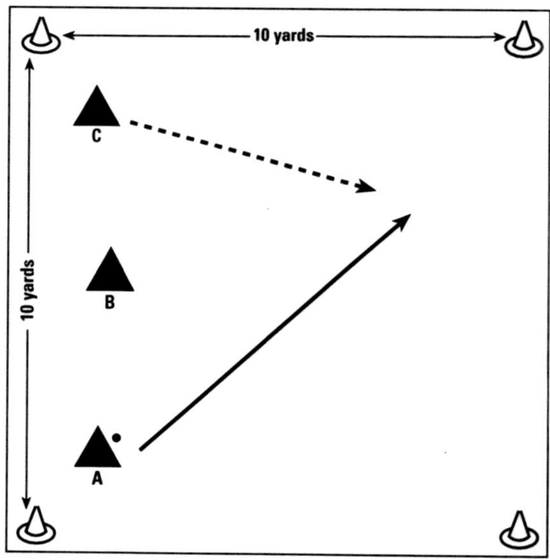

Drill #47: Beat-the-Clock

Objective: To help develop passing and collecting skills with game-like defensive pressure.

Equipment Needed: One soccer ball for every two players, four game markers, two sets of jerseys (one jersey for each player)

Description:

- Divide the group into two equal teams with different jerseys.
- Position team A players, each with a ball, in a 30-yard-by-30-yard grid.
- Members of team B are outside the grid.
- On the coach's signal, players on team B enter the grid, they go to a support position so that teammates can pass them a ball.
- After a team A player has his ball kicked out of the grid, he goes to a support position so that a teammate can pass him a ball.
- The coach times how long it takes the defensive team to get all the balls out of the grid.
- Then the teams switch roles.

Coaching Points: Team A players should move to open space to maintain possession of the ball. Should they lose possession, they should move to a support position where they will try to collect, look, and make a good decision as to where to play the ball next.

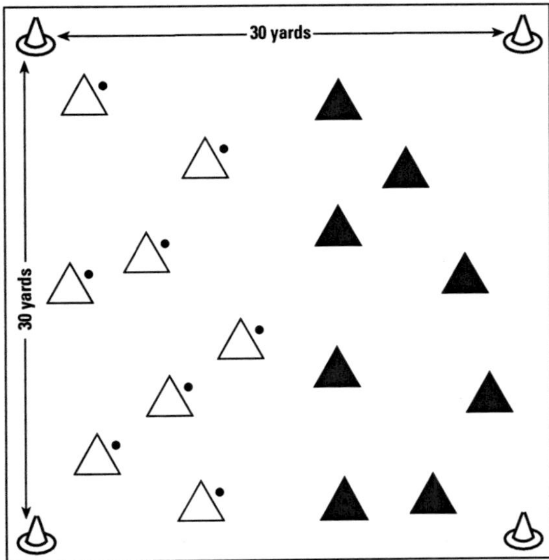

Drill #48: Toss-to-Self Heading

Objective: To help develop the skill of striking the ball with the part of the forehead known as the hairline, with no defensive pressure.

Equipment Needed: One foam or beach ball for every player

Description:

Level 1

- Position players in a scattered formation.
- Players should be on their knees, each with a ball. Players toss the ball slightly above their heads, strike it gently with their heads, and then catch the ball before it strikes the ground.
- Repeat several times.

Level 2

- After players have demonstrated correct heading techniques, have them repeat this action from a standing position.

Coaching Points: Visually demonstrate to players the location of the hairline. Emphasize moving the head to strike the ball instead of merely positioning the head so the ball will hit it. Insist that players strike the ball with their eyes open and mouths closed, which will prevent them from biting their tongues later, when using a harder ball. At Level 2, encourage players to establish a good base of support by slightly flexing their knees and positioning their feet a little more than shoulder-width apart.

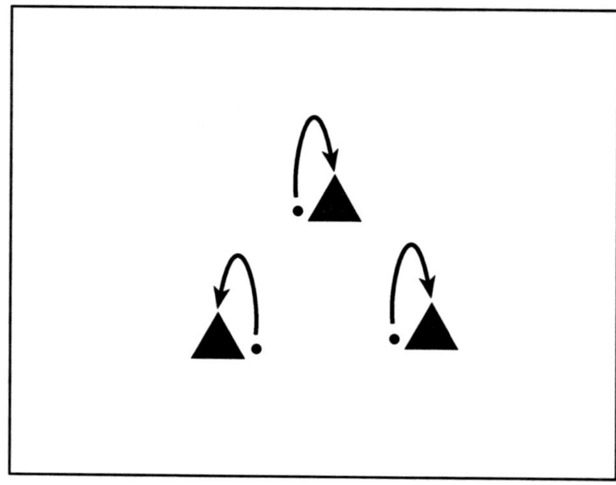

Drill #49: Partner Heading

Objective: To help develop proper heading technique with no defensive pressure.

Equipment Needed: One foam, sponge, or beach ball for every two players and four game markers

Description:

Level 1

- Position players in a 30-yard-by-30-yard grid with a partner.
- Each set of players has a ball.
- The player with the ball tosses to himself and heads the ball to his partner, who will catch, toss, and head it back.

Level 2

- Instead of tossing to himself, the player tosses to his partner, who returns the ball by heading.
- Players should be about five yards apart to begin this phase.
- Gradually increase distance as both tossing and heading skills improve.

Level 3

- The partner tosses to the player in motion, who returns the ball by heading.
- The player in motion should vary directions forward, backward, left, and right.

Coaching Points: Partners should select a type of ball with which they feel comfortable. Emphasize bending at the waist in a backward direction and then thrusting forward to contact the ball to generate more force. Players should flex knees and extend arms to improve balance.

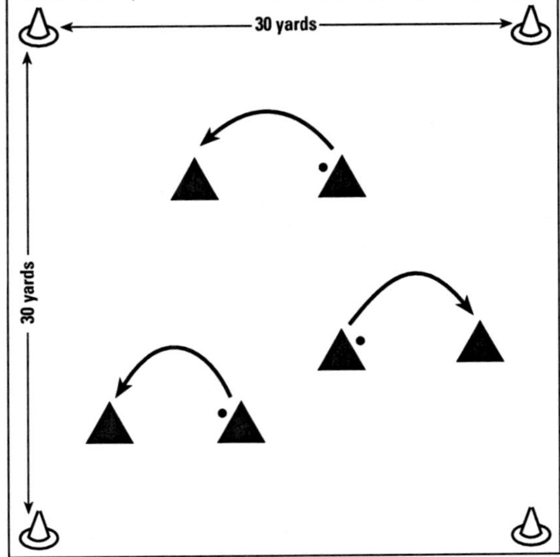

Drill #50: Short and Long Heading

Objective: To help develop force relationships when heading with no defensive pressure.

Equipment Needed: Two soccer balls and four game markers for every three players

Description:

Level 1

- Position three players in a 10-yard-by-10-yard grid.
- Players B and C each have a ball.
- Player B takes a position five yards from player A. Player B tosses to player A, who returns the ball by heading. Player C, who takes a position 10 yards from player A, then tosses, and player A repeats the heading action.

Level 2

- After the first toss, only heading skills are allowed.
- Player B tosses to player A.
- Player A heads to player C.
- Player C heads to player A, who returns the ball by heading to player B.
- Repeat this action.

Coaching Points: Players will need to generate different amounts of force because of the varying distances the ball must travel. Emphasize that the speed with which the head strikes the ball is the major factor in generating this force. Players can increase head speed by bending at the waist and thrusting the upper body forward. At Level 2, use only one ball. Encourage players to move their feet to get good position for striking the ball.

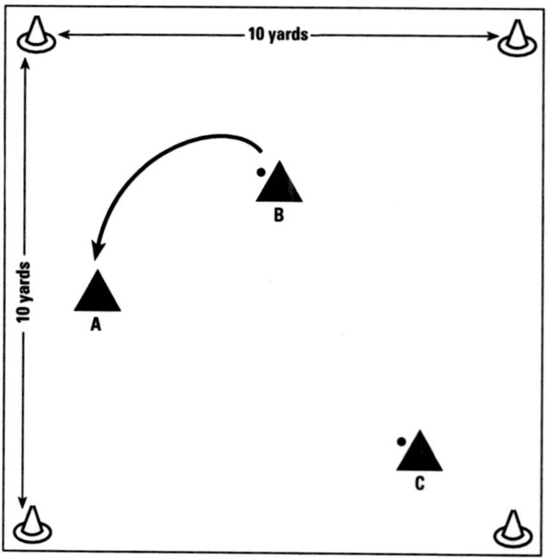

Afterword

After reading this book, I hope you have a better understanding of what soccer is all about, the pitfalls that lie ahead, and how to avoid them whether you are a first-time coach, a veteran coach, a player, or a parent. The most important thing I have learned in my 30-plus years of coaching kids is that if I am true to my values, morals, and well-being, everything will fall into place. Sometimes, it may look as if everything you're doing is wrong, but if you can be flexible and hang in there, all will be okay.

Never lie to kids! They can see through a phony better than anyone. If you lie to them one time, they will never trust you again. Always remember that soccer is fun. Most parents will not have a clue about what you are trying to do, although they might think they do. So, if you keep it fun, the kids—the most important people—will have a good time, learn a few things, and have some great memories—and so will you. I coached a girl from the time she was 8 until she was 12 years of age, and at her high school graduation, she said to me, "Coach Thompson, I just wanted you to know that even though you were a hard coach and made us do drills and run and stuff, I never learned more or had more fun than when I played for you." This girl went on to Harvard and played soccer until she was 21 years old. Harvard ran out of math classes for her. Someday, she will find a cure for cancer or AIDS, I'm sure of it. This kind of success is what coaches live for.

A reporter once asked me, "What do you want your players to say about you after they have moved on?" After thinking about it, I answered, "I hope the players I coached will take with them a love for competition. I hope they will feel I was fair. I know they will think I was tough, demanding, and sometimes hard on them, but I hope they will understand that it was all in the search for excellence within their own ability. But, the most important thing I would want them to say is that they had *fun*!"

Fun is what coaching kids is all about. It doesn't matter if it's soccer, basketball, softball, hockey, track, swimming, or field hockey. The one common thread should be that we, as coaches, must make it fun. Today's athletes are faster, stronger, and in better condition than we ever were. They are smarter, and they have more options than we ever dreamed of. In fact, today, if these athletes can dream it, their dreams will probably happen in their lifetime. Today's athletes are more knowledgeable about conditioning, diet, and training, and as a group, they have a greater understanding of tactical play.

However, today's athletes lack knowledge, which is where coaches can make a difference. The history of the game is being lost through the minutia of the skills and drills our players perform. Coaches must teach today's athletes the history of the game, as well as the skills they need to succeed. Today's athletes need to know how and why they are allowed to play in such outstanding facilities and where the sport has been, as well as where it may be going. Young boys need to hear about past pioneers, such as Kyle Rote, Jr., Ty Keogh, Werner Roth, and Pelé. Young girls need to know about the struggles the women players have had to be recognized as athletes, the victories that have been won, Title IX, and why the names of Mia Hamm, Kristine Lilly, and Michelle Akers mean so much.

Webster's dictionary defines fun as lively, joyous play for amusement, sport, recreation, enjoyment, or pleasure. For the boys and girls, fun is playing soccer, learning new and exciting drills, techniques, and skills every day, meeting new friends, and seeing old acquaintances. Fun is scoring a goal or making a great defensive play. Fun is showing up at practice early to work on corner kicks, staying late with the coach to work on a new drill, hanging out with all the boys or girls before a tournament game, and playing Marco Polo in the pool and elevator tag in the hotel. Fun is hearing your name called as a gold medal is placed around your neck and playing beach soccer with friends just because you like the game. Fun is tournaments and more tournaments, collecting patches from other teams' players, and making the finals, as you finally realize what bonus points mean. Fun is hitting the ball just right with your laces and then looking at the crowd to see the happy faces. Fun is juggling a ball 10 times in a row and heading the ball (when it doesn't hurt). Fun is making a run the full length of the field for the very first time and making a move you've learned and having it work.

Fun, for a coach, can be as simple as the look on a player's face when he first gets to play and the hugs of thanks at the end of the day. Fun is watching your daughter as she grows, learns, and develops new skills and seeing your son play in a field turned to mud by the rain. Fun is watching your 9-year-old daughter catch the ball as a keeper and cheering for your 13-year-old son as he makes a great save as sweeper. Fun is wins, losses, and the occasional tie. Fun is games in the rain and under a clear blue sky. Fun is watching a 9-year-old player try a new move and helping him reach way down, deep inside to master it. Fun is the smiles and the tears, the anxiety and fears, and then when your day is done, it's time to pick up your bag and go home.

About the Author

Howie Thompson is the head soccer coach and director of women's sports at Southeastern Community College in Whiteville, North Carolina. Previously, he coached for 20 years in Connecticut at several high schools and started the Weston Girls Soccer Program in Weston, Connecticut. He also coached at three high schools in the Triangle area of North Carolina and a high school in South Carolina as well. He is the current tournament director for Long Bay Soccer Club in South Carolina and the past tournament director for the Can Am Cup in Myrtle Beach, South Carolina, and helped organize CoastFA Soccer Club in 2006. He is the author of two fiction novels, *A Game for All Seasons*, the story of a young girls' soccer team, and *Overtime*, a story of basketball, love lost and found, and redemption. Howie has three NSCAA/Adidas Regional Coach of the Year awards and was the NSCAA/Adidas 2002 National Coach of the Year. He was awarded the 2003 Who's Who in American Teachers by NSCAA and achieved his National Coaching Diploma in 2006. The motto of Howie's coaching career has been threefold: to help kids, to help kids have fun, and to have fun helping kids.